· THE GREAT ART CITIES OF ITALY ·

ROME · VENICE · FLORENCE NAPLES · POMPEII
Siena and Pisa

LOZZI Roma
edizioni turistiche

Direzione e redazione:
LOZZI ROMA sas
Via Filippo Nicolai, 91 - 00136 ROMA
Tel. 06 35497051 - Tel. e Fax 06 35497074
e-mail: lozzirm@spinweb.it

LE CITTÀ D'ARTE IN ITALIA
Supplemento n° 08 al periodico annuale ROMA LA CITTÀ ETERNA
Reg. Trib. di Roma n° 625 del 13/12/96

Direttore responsabile:
Monica Capuani

Stampato presso la tipografia F. GARRONI
Via Prospero Santacroce, 47 - Roma

Fotolito TIPOCROM srl
Via Gian Galeazzo Arrivabene, 24/38 - Roma

Fotografie:
Archivio fotografico LOZZI ROMA s.a.s.
Le fotografie alle pagine 3-7-21-23 (in basso a sinistra) sono state gentilmente offerte dalla Rolo Banca 1473
Archivio fotografico della Fabbrica di San Pietro
Archivio fotografico Scala
Archivio fotografico Musei e Gallerie Pontificie
Archivio fotografico dell'Osservatore Romano

Computer Mapping: Barbara Cipriani

Aerial view of the Capitol.

ROME

According to tradition, Rome was founded in 753 BC by Romulus, who became its first king. Over a thousand years passed from its birth to its decline following the barbarian invasions. What we admire today in almost every angle of the city center are vestiges from the Republican period, which began with the overthrow of king Tarquinius Superbus in 509 BC, and above all from the subsequent Imperial period, which lasted from Augustus (29 AD) to Romulus Augustus (476 AD).

More than 2750 years of history have not cancelled the traces left by time. Imperial Rome appears before us with all of its magnificence in the area of the Roman Forum, the Palatine Hill and the Colosseum. In fact, the Imperial Age was one of the most exciting periods of Roman culture.

On the artistic and urbanistic level, this was the era in which the Empire began to celebrate itself. The triumphal arches, extraordinary monuments, and the ever-more astounding Imperial Fora exalted the greatness of Rome and its emperors, who were deified after death, and therefore buried in mausoleums of unprecedented commemorative grandiosity.

Rome caput mundi (center of the world), a metropolis with more than one million inhabitants by the end of the 2nd century, reached its greatest splendour under the Flavians, who built the Colosseum, the Baths of Titus, the Palace of Domitian, the Stadium of Domitian (now Piazza Navona) and other buildings which still amaze those who admire them today.

Rome, the Eternal City, has different souls. The magnificence of Imperial Rome is flanked by that of Christian Rome, which was born from it. It was in fact a Roman Emperor, Constantine (4th century AD) who initiated the construction of the first great Christian basilicas: San Giovanni in Laterano, San Lorenzo Fuori le Mura and above all San Pietro in Vaticano. The basilicas of Santa Maria Maggiore and San Paolo were built in the following century.

The celebration of the spiritual and temporal superiority of the Christian world led to Rome's urban Renaissance, which showed its first signs in the middle ages and took firm hold in the early 15th century. From that time on all the popes sought to increase the magnificence of their reign; for example, Nicholas V ordered Bramante to demolish St. Peter's basilica (built in the time of Constantine) and build a new one, and Julius II and Leo X sponsored works by Michelangelo and Raphael.

From the second half of the 15th century, the persistence of the Church's great influence on the European courts gave impulse to a florid urban rebirth, which saw the rise of the great noble palaces, the reconstruction of the Campidoglio (entrusted to Michelangelo by Pope Paul III in 1536), the construction of villas with gardens, piazzas such as Campo de' Fiori and Piazza Farnese, streets like the Via Giulia, and a new network of urban roads on the orders of Pope Sixtus V. The Renaissance architectural model followed classical examples, which were centred on the exactness of rigid geometrical proportions.

In the 17th century, artists broke off from the rigid Renaissance canons. Although it drew some inspiration from classical models, the magnificent, scenographic Roman Baroque dynamically reinterpreted them, giving space to creativity and an abundance of decorative elements. Bernini and Borromini, both Baroque architects, gave new forms to the city's fountains, facades, churches and piazzas, such as the spectacular Piazza Navona.

The 18th century was characterised instead by the creation of works of strong urbanistic impact, among them the Trevi Fountain (1732) and the Spanish Steps (1735).

In the early years of the 19th century, the Baroque passed to the simpler forms of the Neoclassical period on the wave of the rediscovery of classical antiquity in all its forms; the sculpture of Canova, the initiation of systematic archeological excavations and the urban works of Valadier (such as the redesign of Piazza del Popolo and the Pincio Gardens) are only a few examples.

The proclamation of Rome as the capital of the newly unified kingdom of Italy in 1870 brought radical change. The arrival of the royal court, the parliament and government departments led to an immediate rise in the population and upset the tranquil manner of the papal city. In the aftermath of Italian unification, from the end of the 19th century to the first decades of the 20th century, works such as the Vittorio Emanuele II Monument, Palazzo Montecitorio and Piazza della Repubblica were unveiled. The predominant style of the period was the Neo-Renaissance matched with Liberty (Art Deco) and the ever-popular Neoclassicism.

Soon after, the imperialistic aspirations of the fascist regime generated architectural models inspired by ancient Rome. In this period, medieval and Renaissance neighborhoods were destroyed to make way for new boulevards like the Via dei Fori Imperiali and the Via della Conciliazione. At the same time, the expansion plan of the city toward the sea was approved and, as part of this project, the EUR quarter was built.

Today the chaotic growth of the 1950s and 1960s seems to have been halted, and the city has again become the object of renewed attention. Although building new structures compatible with three thousand years of history remains difficult, important campaigns are being developed to honour and preserve the artistic, archeological and human heritage of the city.

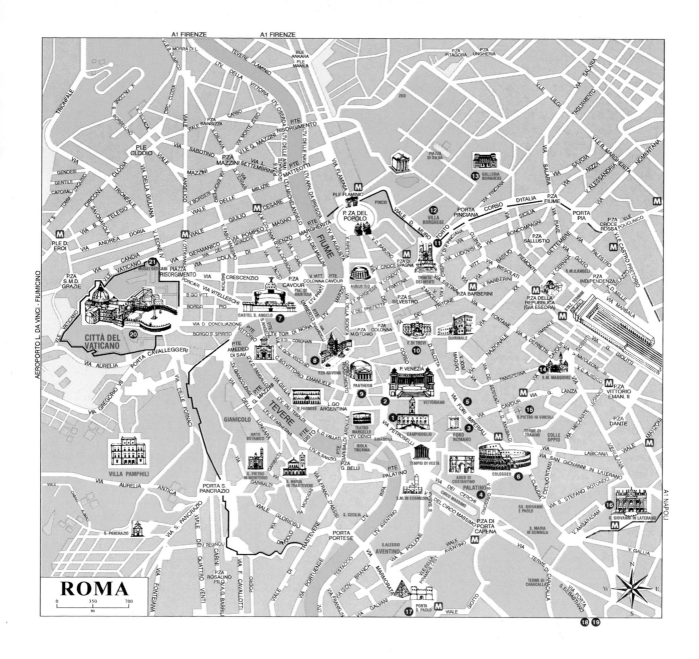

LIST OF THE MONUMENTS

1) The Capitol Hill.
2) Piazza Venezia
3) The Roman Forum.
4) The Palatine Hill.
5) The Imperial Fora.
6) The Colosseum.
7) Castel Sant'Angelo.
8) Piazza Navona.

9) The Pantheon.
10) The Trevi Fountain.
11) Piazza di Spagna.
12) Villa Borghese.
13) The Borghese Gallery and Museum.
14) Santa Maria Maggiore
15) St. Peter in Chains.

16) The Basilica of St. John in the Lateran.
17) St. Paul outside the Walls.
18) The Catacombs.
19) Via Appia Antica.
20) St. Peter's Basilica.
21) The Vatican Museums and Sistine Chapel.

ROME

THE CAPITOL HILL AND CAPITOLINE MUSEUMS

At the top of the celebrated Capitoline Hill is the **Piazza del Campidoglio**, which bears the mark of the artistic genius of Michelangelo, who redesigned it for the triumphal visit of the Emperor Charles V in 1536. The piazza was already the site of the medieval **Palazzo Senatorio** and the **Tabularium** of ancient Rome, yet Michelangelo planned an extraordinarily harmonious complex, with a new facade and double staircase for Palazzo Senatorio (still the seat of the mayor and Town Council). He then projected the facades of the lateral buildings, the Palazzo dei Conservatori and the Palazzo Nuovo, at slightly converging angles. Michelangelo never saw the completion of this project.

The *facade* of **Palazzo dei Conservatori** was built by Giacomo della Porta, with some modifications, in 1563; **Palazzo Nuovo** was completed by Girolamo Rainaldi in the mid- 17th century to hold the works of art that Palazzo dei Conservatori was not able to contain.

Inside Palazzo Nuovo is a beautiful courtyard with a *fountain* surmounted by a colossal statue of an ocean god, known by the name *Marforio*. On the right, behind a glass wall, is the original *equestrian statue of the Emperor Marcus Aurelius* in gilded bronze (161 - 180 AD), which dominated Piazza del Campidoglio from 1538. On the first floor, the long gallery, flanked by a series of "theme" rooms, reflects the archeological taste of the 18th century, the period in which the museum was set up: a forest of sculpture as far as the eye can see.

On the right of the Gallery is the *Sala delle Colombe* (Room of the Doves), with the beautiful mosaic found at Hadrian's Villa in Tivoli. Further ahead is the *Capitoline Venus*, whose harmonious beauty is enhanced by the sober fusion of lines and colors of the octagonal chamber in which it stands. The rooms which follow are rich with statues realised in Roman portrait style.

The courtyard of the Palazzo dei Conservatori, seat of the **Capitoline Museums**, contains sculptures of enormous dimensions, among which are the remains of a colossal *statue of the Emperor Constantine*. On the first floor are the *Sala degli Orazi e Curiazi*, *Sala dei Capitani*, *Sala dei Trionfi Romani* and the *Sala della Lupa*, the last of which contains the *Capitoline Wolf*, a 4th-century BC bronze statue which is the symbol of Rome. The twins, Romulus and Remus, were added at the beginning of the 16th century by the sculptor Antonio Pollaiolo.

The **Capitoline Picture Gallery** includes important masterpieces of the 16th and the 17th centuries, among them: *Romulus and Remus* by Rubens, *Anthony and Cleopatra* by Guercino, the *Rape of Helena* by Paolo Veronese, *St. Sebastian* by Guido Reni, the *Magdalene* by Tintoretto, the *Gypsy who foretells the future* and *St. John the Baptist* by Caravaggio, and portraits by Van Dyck.

1) Removing a thorn. 2) Love and Psyche 3) Remains of the colossal statue of Constantine. 4) St. John by Caravaggio. 5) The Esquiline Venus. 6) Dying Gaul.

PIAZZA VENEZIA

The piazza takes its name from **Palazzo Venezia**, Rome's first palace in the classic Renaissance style, which Cardinal Pietro Barbo (later Pope Paul II) had redesigned in its present form in 1455, incorporating the tower and other preexisting medieval elements.

The palace, and in particular the balcony which opens onto the center of the facade, acquired great notoriety in this century for other than artistic reasons: from there the fascist leader Mussolini addressed the crowds below.

Dominating the piazza is the white and grandiose **Victor Emanuel II Monument**, more commonly called the "*Vittoriano*," built between 1885 and 1911 by the architect Giuseppe Sacconi. At the top of the marble stairs is the *Tomb of the Unknown Soldier*, consecrated after World War I (1915-1918) in honour of the hundreds of thousands of fallen Italian soldiers.

THE ROMAN FORUM

Meeting point of idlers as well as seat of the highest Roman institutions; center of petty, everyday commerce as well as of the courts, with the coming and going of prosecutors, lawyers and judges; theatre of gladiator games and at the same time background crowded with temples and honourary monuments for the great triumphs of victorious generals: all this was, in the long centuries of its history, the **Forum**, heart of the Roman Republic.

When the people living on the surrounding hillsides, and above all, those coming from the Palatine Hill (the future Rome) began to use the valley below as a meeting place and market, they decided to drain and pave the area to make it healthier. Little remains from the monarchical period, however, apart from legend. During the Republican era (6th to 1st century BC), the Forum was enriched by ever more splendid structures, which outlined the progressive transfor-

Aerial view of the Fora and of Piazza Venezia with the Monument to Victor Emanuel II.

mation of Rome from an Italic village into the most important metropolis in the ancient Mediterranean world.

With the arrival of the Empire (27 AD), the glorious Republican Forum lost its role as the political center of the city, despite the fact that it continued to be adorned by temples and increasingly bulkier monuments amassed in an ever-narrowing space. Meanwhile, in the vicinity, the first emperors built new fora, of an honourary and celebratory significance much different than that of the Republican Forum. With the fall of the Roman Empire (476 AD), the fora were progressively abandoned.

Entering from the Via dei Fori Imperiali gate, on the right are the remains of the **Basilica Emilia**, built in the 2nd century AD as a civil court. A few fragments of finely worked marble of various dimension are still visible. The following building is the apparently intact **Curia**, ancient seat of the Roman Senate. Destroyed and rebuilt many times, it was transformed in the middle ages into a Christian church dedicated to St. Hadrian, and in the 1930s restored to its original appearance. On display *inside* are two splendid reliefs, the so-called *Plutei of Trajan*, two sculpted parapets with scenes of ceremonies held in the Forum.

Much more recent is the beautifully proportioned **Arch of Septimius Severus**, with three barrel-vaults, whose inscriptions bear the memory of an Imperial tragedy: dedicated in 203 AD by the Emperor to himself and his children Geta and Caracalla, the name of Geta was cancelled after he was killed by his brother in a struggle for succession.

Above, against the edge of the Capitoline Hill is the grandiose **Tabularium**, state archive of the Roman Republic. Higher up is the Palazzo Senatorio, which dominates the vast valley of the Forum.

Three Corinthian columns surmounted by a finely decorated cornice are what remains of the **Temple of Vespasian**, built in 81 AD. At the central area of the Forum, at the height of the *Rostrum*, on the Via Sacra, are the imposing ionic columns of the *Temple of Saturn*, first built in the 5th century BC, and rebuilt many times after. It served as the treasury of the Roman people, for centuries holding enormous quantities of gold.

On the right, turning away from the Campidoglio, on the *Via Nova*, is the **Basilica Julia**, built by Julius Caesar in the middle of the 1st century AD. It was divided into sections with movable partitions which allowed the grandiose building to be used for several hearings simultaneously.

On the same axis of the Basilica is the **Temple of Castor**

The Roman Forum.

The Roman Forum seen from the Campidoglio.

The Roman Forum. To the right is the Arch of Septimius Severus; in the background the Tabularium and the Campidoglio.

and Pollux, dedicated to the mythical twins who were the legendary protectors of Rome. First built in the 5th century BC, it was rebuilt in the age of Augustus. Only three columns on a high pediment remain standing.

One side of the oblong trapezoid of the central area of the Forum is delineated by the **Temple of Julius Caesar**. Built on the site where the body of Caesar was cremated, it is the first example of the process of Imperial deification that characterised the successive period. The temple marks the end of the first and oldest monumental nucleus of the Forum.

Continuing toward the Arch of Titus, we find the harmonious round **Temple of Vesta** and the **House of the Vestals**, servants of the goddess Vesta. The temple, one of the oldest and most venerated in the city, was almost entirely rebuilt by the Emperor Septimius Severus after a fire in 191 AD, as was the adjacent house of the sacerdotal priestesses, the remains of which give us an idea of the daily life of this community.

On the *Via Sacra*, we come before the **Temple of Antoninus and Faustina**, the 2nd century AD emperor and his wife. It is one of the best-preserved buildings in the Forum, due to its transformation into the church of *San Lorenzo in Miranda*, which preserved the elegant facade of the original structure. To the side rises the **round Temple of Romulus**, dedicated not to the mythical founder of Rome, but to the son of the Emperor Maxentius, who died in 309 AD and was

obviously deified. The exceptionally well-preserved bronze doors of the temple still feature the original lock.

Ahead on the left is the **Basilica of Maxentius**, or **Constantine**, begun by the first and finished by his victorious rival at the beginning of the 4th century AD. Like others outside the original nucleus of the Forum, the basilica dates to the late Imperial period. A good portion of the building is no longer visible, as it was used as a mine for building materials over the centuries.

At the apex of the Via Sacra, the elegant **Arch of Titus**, with its slender, single barrel-vault, makes a fitting end for the visit to the Forum. Beyond its historical importance (it commemorates, in fact, the victory of the Emperor over the Jews in 70 AD, which began the Diaspora of the Jewish people), the arch is noteworthy for the artistic quality of its reliefs. Among the most beautiful of Roman sculptures, they were inspired by the pictorial panels of battle scenes which victorious Roman generals showed the festive crowds during triumphal marches along the Via Sacra.

On the left, in front of the Colosseum, we find the ruins of the **Temple of Venus and Roma**, built in honour of the two goddesses and designed by the Emperor Hadrian in 135 AD. It was the largest temple in Rome, with the part dedicated to Venus on a high platform (still visible) extending toward the Colosseum.

Aerial view of the Palatine and Roman Forum.

THE PALATINE HILL

From the moment of the legendary founding of Rome, when Romulus "traced a furrowed square", until the birth of the Empire, the Palatine Hill changed very little: only a few sacred areas and isolated dwellings of illustrious families were hidden in the greenery at its sides. Its destiny changed when Augustus became Emperor and chose the Palatine Hill as the site of his Imperial residence. His successors, one after another, erected ever-more vast Imperial palaces. Then came the oblivion of the long centuries of the middle ages, followed by the reawakening of the Renaissance, when the grandiose **Villa Farnese** with its still splendid **Giardini** or **Orti Farnesiani** (Farnese Gardens) was built. The latter were the first botanical gardens in the world. Underneath them extends the *Loggia of Tiberius,* built by the first successor to Augustus.

The residential area associated with the first Roman Emperor was made up of the so-called **House of Livia** (his wife) and the **House of Augustus**. The first, excavated in 1869, is in fairly good condition and contains an original mosaic floor, interesting wall murals, some pic-torial decoration in the central room (*tablinum*), with mythical subjects framed in an architectural perspective. Tiberius, the successor to Augustus, built the Palatine's first true royal palace, the **Domus Tiberiana**, still interred below the 16th century Farnese Gardens.

The magnificence of the grandiose Imperial palaces built by the Flavians was meant to underline the return of the emperors to the traditional seat of the Palatine Hill after Nero's incredible undertaking, the immense Domus Aurea (Golden House).

The **Palatine Antiquarium**, at the center of the hill, was reopened in 1997. *Inside* are numerous interesting relics from excavations around the fora. To the left extend the ruins of the official part of the royal residence, called the **Flavian Palace**. On the right are the ruins of the private portion, called the **Domus Augustana**, still partially unexplored. At the side of the Domus is an unexpected and stunning sight: the huge **Stadium of Domitian** or *Hippodrome*, a final addition worthy of the royal residence, built by the architect Rabirio at the end of the 1st century AD. Beyond the Stadium, between the 2nd and 3rd centuries, the Emperor Septimius Severus built the *septizodium*, the last of the mighty Imperial residences on the Palatine.

THE IMPERIAL FORA

The Imperial Fora flank the first part of the road that connects Piazza Venezia with Piazza del Colosseo. It is essential to use all of our imagination to reconstruct this inseparable group of five majestic monumental squares, built between the 1st century BC and the 1st century AD., by Caesar, Augustus, Domitian, Nerva and Trajan, respectively.

The first of the Imperial Fora on the right is the **Forum of Caesar**, begun by the Roman leader immediately after his conquest of Gaul, when the booty was used to embellish Rome. Work started in 51 BC, according to a plan which presented two fundamental novelties: the closure of the piazza by a perimeter wall and the location of the principle temple, dedicated to the founder, on the side opposite the entrance. In this way the Forum was transformed into a monumental celebratory complex, which anticipated the deification of the figure of the Emperor. Three Corinthian columns remain from the *Temple*, dedicated to *Venus Genetrix* and rebuilt at the time of Trajan.

On the opposite side of the Via dei Fori Imperiali we find the **Forum of Trajan**. For its construction, the Emperor had to make use of the limited remaining area between the Quirinal Hill, which he partially excavated, and the Campidoglio. The **column** that stands in the center of the area shows the previous ground level of the Qurinal Hill, as remembered in an inscription in the base. This splendid work of sculpture, with figures in relief, shows episodes from Trajan's conquest of Dacia (modern-day Romania).

The **Basilica Ulpia,** *the Greek and Latin Libraries and the pronaos* of the temple dedicated to the Emperor created a sort of square courtyard around the column. Everything was contained inside a vast porticoed enclosure, which opened the majestic entrance to the forum, made up of a triumphal arch with just one vault.

The forum of Trajan is scenographically completed by **Trajan's Markets**, which rest against the edge of the Quirinal Hill. Surprisingly well-preserved, the semi-circle with several floors could be compared with a modern-day commercial center, with shops and halls for public assembly. Continuing along the Via dei Fori Imperiali in the direction of the Colosseum, after Trajan's Forum we come to the **Forum of Augustus**. The *Temple*, dedicated to *Mars Ultor*, rises from a high podium; following the scheme of the Forum of Caesar it was placed at the back of the piazza, which constitutes the only portion of the complex still visible.

On the side, little remains of the **Forum of Nerva**, actually begun by Domitian and completed by Nerva in 97 AD. It was dominated by the *Temple of Minerva*, the imposing remains of which were visible until the 17th century, when the marble was used to build the famous Fontana Paola on the Janiculum Hill.

The Trajan's Markets by night.

Trajan's Forum and Trajan's Column. To the right, Trajan's Markets.

The Trajan's Markets. In the background the Monument to Victor Emanuel II.

THE COLOSSEUM

Before approaching the Colosseum, we pause in the piazza which occupies the valley of this imposing structure, on the side of the Arch of Constantine. Important excavation work has revealed precious remains, which for the most part date to the time of Nero (who died eleven years before the Colosseum was built), when this was the site of a small artificial lake which completed the spectacular park of the Domus Aurea.

The area of the excavations reaches as far as the **Arch of Constantine**, the greatest of the three surviving triumphal arches. Its inscription recalls the victory of Constantine over his rival Maxentius in 312 AD, and, with an allusion to an abstract "divinity" in place of the usual gods of pagan Olympus, the incipient triumph of Christianity. The arch is made up of elements added in different periods through the beginning of the 4th century, when the two medallions on the short sides were sculpted, along with the friezes on the side arches (the scene of the Battle of the Milvian Bridge among them) and the bases of the columns, which are the only parts made especially for the arch.

We now turn our attention to one of the great protagonists of monumental Rome, the *Flavian Amphitheater* or **Colosseum**, built by the Flavian emperors to host the public games. It was finished in just a few years, thanks to the simultaneous work of four building yards, one in each of the quadrants into which the site was divided.

The *exterior* of the Colosseum, even if stripped, mutilated (only about half of the original structure remains) and held up by two buttresses, still preserves all the clear beauty of its original design, which exalted the most significant feature of Roman architecture: the matching of arch and architrave.

The dimensions of the monument are eloquent: the elliptical plan measures 188 meters at its greater axis, 156 in its shorter axis, and reached a height of about 50 meters. According to documentary evidence and complex calculations, it accommodated eighty thousand spectators.

The system of public access was extremely efficient: the external arches had numbers (some still visible today), which corresponded to the spectators' tickets.

Naturally, the interior is today much different than it was originally. Little remains of the *cavea*, divided in five levels. The first level of seating, reserved for senators, was lined with marble; successive levels in stone; the last level, reserved for Roman women, in wood.

The functional *subterranean* levels are now exposed, but were once covered by the floor of the arena, made up of a wooden platform.

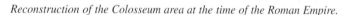

Reconstruction of the Colosseum area at the time of the Roman Empire.

Aerial view of the Coloseum, with the Roman Forum in the background.

The Colosseum.

The Arch of Constantine.

Aerial view of Castel Sant'Angelo.

CASTEL SANT'ANGELO

Castel Sant'Angelo is reached by crossing the beautiful **Ponte Sant'Angelo**, a bridge rendered spectacular by ten statues of angels with the symbols of the Passion of Christ, made between 1667 and 1669 according to designs by Bernini.

Beyond the bridge, Castel Sant'Angelo appears to be an impenetrable, fortified bastion, but originally it was built to hold the mortal remains of the Emperor Hadrian. The *Hadrianeum* or Hadrian's Mausoleum was begun by Hadrian himself in 130 AD and finished in 139 AD, a year after his death.

The original structure of the mausoleum is still the central fulcrum of the castle. The castle-fortress was characterised by its strategic role during the entire middle ages. In the 13th century it was connected to the Vatican Palaces by a passageway, "il passetto", above the Leonine walls. This underlines the castle's close connection with the Vatican, for which it was a true haven for centuries. Inside, several parts belong to the original mausoleum: the ample *vaulted vestibule*; the *heliocoidal ramp*, along which the tiny, inhospitable *celle* (cells) which held prisoners can be seen; the huge *central room*, destined to contain the funerary urn of the Emperor Hadrian and his descendants. This last part is crossed by the Renaissance *Cordonata di Alessandro VI* which cuts across the entire structure.

The levels of the courtyards are primarily Renaissance in character. The *Cortile d'Onore* or *dell'Angelo* (Courtyard of honour, or of the Angel) is dominated by the facade of the *Chapel of Pope Leo X*, designed by Michelangelo.

Climbing the nearby stairs to the right of the entrance of the *Cortile del Teatro* or *del Pozzo* (Courtyard of the Theatre, or of the Well) is the *bathroom of Pope Clement VI*, a small room decorated by Giulio Romano, one of the best students of Raphael. A walkway encircling the castle begins from the airy *Loggia di Giulio II*, which offers one of the most celebrated (with good reason) panoramas of Rome. A few steps away are the *Papal Apartments*, built around the mid-16th century for Pope Paul III, with a succession of richly decorated and furnished rooms. The castle is surmounted by the *Angelo*, the archangel Michael, made in 1753 by Pieter Verschaffelt.

PIAZZA NAVONA

Piazza Navona is probably the most significant site of Baroque Rome. Its beautiful oblong form follows the lay-out of the *Stadium of Domitian;* although plundered, it remained mostly intact until 1477, when Pope Sixtus IV moved the market here from the Campidoglio. The definitive 17th-century look we admire today is owed to the sovereign of the Baroque age, Gian Lorenzo Bernini, and to his ever-present rival Francesco Borromini. The first is responsible for the design of the central axis of the piazza, with the three scenographic fountains, among which the most important is the central **Fountain of the Four Rivers**, built to hold up the obelisk found at the Circus of Romulus or Maxentius on the Appian Way. The allegorical figures of the Danube, the Nile, the Ganges and the Rio de la Plata made by Bernini's followers, representing the parts of the known world, are placed on a crag (originally coloured) populated with real and fantastic animals. The two pre-existing lateral fountains harmoniously complete the decor of the piazza, occupying the two foci of the ellipse.

At the center of the west side of the piazza is the church of **Sant'Agnese in Agone**. Begun by Giacomo Rainaldi in 1652 on the order of Pope Innocent X, it was finished by Francesco Borromini, who created the unique concave facade, framed on the sides by two high towers and surmounted by a cupola inspired by Michelangelo.

The Fountain of the Four Rivers.

The Fountain of the Moor.

The Fountain of Neptune.

THE PANTHEON

As the beautiful inscription across the facade suggests, the Pantheon was built by the famous Agrippa, one of Emperor Augustus' principal collaborators. Almost completely destroyed by a fire, it was remade by Hadrian in 118 AD. The building is substantially intact, thanks to the Byzantine Emperor Phocas, who gave the pagan temple to Pope Boniface IV in 608, who then transformed it into a Christian church.

The *facade* has the classical appearance of a Roman temple, with a colonnaded portico surmounted by a triangular front, which over the course of the centuries was used for various contrasting purposes. The traditional pronaos leads to the *interior*, whose round plan makes up the supporting drum for the celebrated cupola. It is actually a cap, whose thickness diminishes as it rises; in the center is an open oculus (8.92 meters in diameter), which features some of the original bronze trim.

The interior is therefore a single majestic space entirely centred on a curved line, highlighted by the clear light which falls from the central oculus, also typical of Roman architecture. Naturally, the statues of the gods which once stood in the large niches have long since been substituted by the *central altar* and the *funeral monuments*, among them that of Raphael. The Pantheon also hosts several tombs of the royal family.

The Pantheon.

Right: Aerial view of Trevi Fountain.

THE TREVI FOUNTAIN

Upon reaching the Piazza di Trevi, the first reaction is one of surprise. The most monumental and celebrated fountain in Rome is contained in an extremely reduced space, which heightens the scenographic effect.

Built for Pope Clement XII between 1732 and 1751 according to plans by Nicola Salvi, the fountain is decorated by rich figures and reliefs above clusters of rocks, over which break thousands of rivulets of water. The god Oceano dominates the scene from a chariot in the form of a shell pulled by sea horses. The entire facade of Palazzo Poli forms the background. The relief on the right shows Agrippa explaining to the Emperor Augustus the plan to bring the Acqua Vergine from its source to Rome via an aqueduct that to this day delivers water to the fountain.

According to an ancient tradition, by tossing a coin into the basin of the fountain, a tourist is assured a return to Rome. A thorough restoration in 1991 brought the fountain back to its original splendour.

PIAZZA DI SPAGNA

This piazza is one of the essential stops for even the most brief visit to Rome. Like many other Roman squares, this irregularly shaped piazza features various architectural styles, but the focus is the celebrated **Scalinata di Trinita' dei Monti**, or Spanish Steps, which harmoniously connect the piazza with the Pincio hill.

At its feet is the *Fountain of the Broken Boat*, attributed to Gian Lorenzo Bernini or his father Pietro. The steps, designed in 1724 by the Roman architect Francesco de Sanctis for the King of France, form a splendid base for the slanting facade of the 16th century *Church of the Trinita' dei Monti*.

The church is flanked by two bell towers by Giacomo della Porta, whose verticality is heightened by the soaring Egyptian obelisk in the center.

The southern end of the piazza is closed by the severe facade of Bernini's *Palazzo di Propaganda Fide*, and the *Baroque Palazzo di Spagna*.

Piazza di Spagna and the Spanish Steps. Below, the Fountain of the Broken Boat.

VILLA BORGHESE

Created by young Cardinal Scipione Borghese at the beginning of the 17th century, Villa Borghese is the green heart of central Rome. Among tree-lined avenues, small lakes and greenery are numerous sites of great artistic and cultural interest, including the Pincio Gardens, designed by Valadier, which offer a splendid view of Rome from a terrace that dominates Piazza del Popolo below; the **Museo Nazionale di Villa Giulia,** inside a beautiful 16th-century building by Vasari, Ammannati and Vignola, rich with Etruscan relics; the **Galleria Borghese**; the **Galleria Nazionale di Arte Moderna** and the *Zoo*.

THE BORGHESE GALLERY AND MUSEUM

The museum and gallery are set in a splendid 17th-century casino, renovated in the 18th century by Prince Marcantonio Borghese to show his prestigious family collection. The casino reopened in 1997 after a very lengthy and thorough restoration. The Museum is arranged on the ground floor and dedicated to sculpture, while the Gallery, on the first floor, contains paintings.

Among the great works are the statue of *Paolina Borghese* as *Venus Venetrix*, the celebrated masterpiece by Antonio Canova (1805); the *David* and the marble group *Apollo and Daphne*, both sculpted in 1624 by Bernini, who also did the *Rape of Proserpina* and the group of *Aeneas and Anchises*. The Roman replica of the *Dancing Faun* is full of life.

Only very few of the hundreds of works of art in the Gallery can be mentioned here: the *Deposition by Raphael* (1507), *St. John the Baptist in the Desert* and the *David with the head of Goliath* by the unmistakable Caravaggio; the *Deposition* by Rubens; *Sacred and Profane Love*, perhaps the jewel of the Gallery, by Titian. Other noteworthy artists represented here include Correggio, Dürer and Salvator Rosa.

The graceful Moses Fountain.

The lake in Villa Borghese Park with its Temple of Aesculapius.

The statue of Paolina Borghese by Canova.

THE BASILICA OF
SANTA MARIA MAGGIORE

The basilica, also called *Liberiana*, is the oldest and largest among those dedicated to the cult of the Virgin Mary. It was built by Sixtus III to celebrate the conclusion of the Council of Ephesus (431).

Although the original structure remains, today the church shows traces of the numerous enlargements, additions and embellishments made over the centuries. The soberly scenographic effect of the *facade* by Ferdinando Fuga is typical of the 18th century. Above it rises the beautiful late-Romanesque 14th-century **campanile** with its pyramidal cusp; at 75 meters, it is the tallest in Rome.

On the *portico*, there are five doors under great architraved openings; the first on the left is the *Porta Santa* (Holy Door), which is only opened together with the Holy Doors at St. Peter's and St. Paul's.

The vast and harmonious *interior* of the basilica is divided in three naves. The enormous *central nave*, with its rich *Renaissance ceiling* and splendid *Cosmatesque pavement* (12th-century) is flanked by a double row of large monolithic columns. But the supreme testimony to the basilica's art and history is the stupendous **Triumphal Arch**, which rises at the end of the nave.

The rich *baldacchino* (canopy), also the work of Ferdinando Fuga, rises under the arch and above the *Main Altar*, in front of which opens the *Cript of the Confession*, where the precious *relics of the Presepe* are kept.

Beyond the main altar, at last, we admire a real apotheosis of mosaic decoration which constitutes the artistic treasure of this basilica: the cap of the *apse*, in fact, is completely decorated by a great *mosaic* of the *Triumph of Mary* by Jacopo Torriti (1295).

In the *right nave* is the *Chapel of the Baptistery*, by Flaminio Ponzio (1605), while the porphyry *baptismal font* is a 19th century work by Luigi Valadier; the *Cappella Sistina* (Sistine Chapel) corresponds to the right arm of the transept and was built by the architect Domenico Fontana, while the corresponding *Cappella Paolina* (Paoline Chapel) named after Pope Paul V who is buried there, fills the left arm of the transept.

The famous St. Peter's Chains.

Michelangelo's powerful sculpture of Moses.

The piazza of St. John in the Lateran.

THE BASILICA OF ST. PETER IN CHAINS
(San Pietro in Vincoli)

This church is also known as the *Basilica Eudossiana*, from the name of the 5th-century empress who, according to tradition, founded the basilica to hold the *chains* (*vincula* in Latin) which once held St. Peter. The *facade* features an elegant late-15th century portico. The *interior* was restored by Domenico Fontana in the 18th century.
At the end of the right nave is one of the most celebrated statues in the world: Michelangelo's **Moses**. The strong figure of the great biblical protagonist is at the center of a funerary monument designed to hold to the tomb of Pope Julius II.

THE BASILICA OF ST. JOHN IN THE LATERAN
(San Giovanni in Laterano)

San Giovanni in Laterano is the Cathedral of the Eternal City. Like St. Peter's and St. Paul's, it was founded at the time of Constantine. Little remains from the early basilica, where the popes resided until 1305.
The *facade* is a masterpiece of 18th-century architecture by Alessandro Galilei, who gave it a new touch: above five great architraved openings stands an order of arcades; the one in the middle, flanked by two pairs of semicolumns and surmounted by a neat tympanum, slightly jutting out. A high balustrade adorned by fifteen statues on

top crowns the building: *Christ* at the center, *Saint John the Baptist* and *St. John the Evangelist* at his sides, followed by the *Twelve Doctors of the Latin and Greek Churches*.

In addition to the *Statue of Constantine* at the extreme left of the *portico*, the five doors corresponding to the five naves into which the basilica is sub-divided are also notable. The *Central Door* dates to Roman times. The last on the right is the *Porta Santa* (Holy Door), connected with the ceremonies of the Jubilee Year.

The vast and majestic *interior* clearly betrays the Baroque hand of Francesco Borromini, who Pope Innocent X entrusted with restoration for the Jubilee year 1650. The pre-existing rich coffered ceiling, featuring inlaid wood and gold, remained untouched. In the *right-side intermediate nave*, along the wall of the first pilaster that divides it from the central nave, is one of the artistic and historic jewels of the basilica; attributed by most scholars to Giotto, the fresco fragment is of particular value to visitors during the Holy Year, as it represents Pope *Boniface VIII proclaiming the Holy Year of 1300*. The *nave on the far left* holds several important chapels and the famous *Monument to Cardinal Annibaldi*, a conspicuously Gothic work, with which Arnolfo di Cambio made his first entrance into the Roman artistic world.

In the center rises the fine late-Gothic *tabernacle*, built in 1367 by the elegant Senese artist Giovanni di Stefano for Pope Urban V. The busts in gilded silver up above, repre-

The Basilica of St. John in the Lateran.

St. John in the Lateran. The papal altar under a canopy built in 1367.

senting *Sts. Peter* and *Paul*, contain venerated *relics* of the two Apostles.

The *Papal Altar* underneath, rebuilt in 1851, holds the unadorned wooden *table* upon which, according to tradition, the first popes (from St. Peter to St. Sylvester I) officiated. In front of the altar is the *confession*, which holds the *Tomb of Martin V*.

The *apse*, remade under the papacy of Leo XIII (1884), enlarged the form of the old basilica, and was decorated by restoring the preexisting late-13th century *mosaics* by Jacopo Torriti and Jacopo da Camerino. The airy **cloister** is the work of the celebrated Roman marble artists of the 13th century, the Vassalletto family, who also did the cloister of the Basilica di San Paolo.

THE BASILICA OF
ST. PAUL OUTSIDE THE WALLS
(San Paolo fuori le Mura)

The church rises over the site of the tomb of St. Paul, and was built by the Emperor Constantine two and a half centuries after the death of the apostle. After enlargements and embellishments by his successors, by the 5th century this was the largest religious building in the Christian world. The splendid construction was destroyed in a few hours by a ruinous fire on the night between July 15th and 16th of 1823. Pope Leo XII promptly ordered the basilica to be rebuilt in 1832. The present church closely follows the plan and dimensions of its predecessor, albeit with a different style.

The main entrance of the basilica, on the side of the Tiber, opens onto the *quadriporticus* (atrium), with an imposing *Statue of the Apostle* standing at the center.

The *facade* faithfully recreates the ancient splendour of the glow of polychrome mosaics against a golden background that once adorned it. The overall effect remains suggestive, with the grandiose figure of the *Benedictory Christ and Sts. Peter and Paul* on the tympanum, while in the middle area the *Agnus Dei* on the Holy Mount stands out. Below are the figures of the *four Prophets*.

After the *Central Door*, the first door on the right is the *Porta Santa* (*Holy Door*), which is opened only for the Holy Year. The *interior* of the basilica is striking, above all for its fantastic luminosity. Two solemn rows of arcades divide the central nave from the side naves (each divided in two by as many columns), surmounted by a long series of *mosaic medallions* portraying the 264 popes, from St. Peter to John Paul II. The *Triumphal Arch,* supported by two granite monolithic columns that stand 14 meters tall, rises from the part opposite the central nave.

At the center of the transept is a 13th-century *ciborio* (canopy) by Arnolfo di Cambio and mosaics in the apse. The *baldacchino* covers the simple *papal altar*, made from porphyry and white marble, which sits on top of the *arca marmorea* (marble arch).

The *apse mosaic* was realised by Venetian artists in the 13th century for Pope Honorius III, who is represented in tiny scale under the figure of the *Benedictory Jesus* between four *Apostles*.

Against the apse and rising above the stupendous polychromatic *floor* sits the *papal chair*, in white marble with precious ornamentation in gilded bronze.

To the right side of the transept is a small complex of rooms and a chapel, which then leads to the **cloister**, designed by Vassalletto and one of the most suggestive in Rome.

THE CATACOMBS

Three complexes of catacombs line the Appian Way: the *Catacombs of San Callisto*, *San Sebastiano* and *Domitilla*. The name "catacomb" originally referred only to the Catacombs of San Sebastiano, a burial place set into the subterranean galleries of a pozzolana mine. With the diffusion of Christianity, which used exclusively the ritual of burial, it became necessary to extend the underground tunnels in various areas, digging out several levels for tens of kilometers. At the most difficult times, the Christians sheltered themselves in the catacombs, trusting that no Roman would ever violate the sanctity of the cemeteries.

On the Appian Way we meet first the **Catacombs of San Callisto**, the oldest official cemetery of the Christian community in Rome, particularly venerated for having held the tombs of almost all the popes of the 3rd century. It is a vast complex that extends over four levels, of particular interest are the *Cripta dei Papi* (Crypt of the Popes) and the *Cripta di Santa Cecilia* (Crypt of St. Cecilia), where the body of the young saint was found miraculously intact.

The nearby **Catacombs of San Sebastiano** is the only Christian cemetery that has always been accessible. They extend in several levels underneath the **Basilica** of the same name, which was built in the 4th century but redecorated in the 17th century by Flaminio Ponzio and Giovanni Vasanzio. Noteworthy parts include the *Cubicolo di Giona*, with an interesting late-4th century fresco decoration, and the *Villa Romana*, decorated with architectural and naturalistic frescoes. Most striking is the so-called *piazzola* (little piazza) which appears unexpectedly at the end of an intricate web of tunnels. *Three Mausoleums* date to the 1st - 2nd century and were first used by pagans as colombari, then by Christians as tombs for burial. There are numerous touching examples of graffiti by the faithful.

The entrance to the **Catacombs of Domitilla** is across a pleasant garden, underneath the beautiful *paleo-christian Basilica of Sts. Nero and Achilles*, rebuilt after having been discovered completely underground in 1874. The fresco in the *Cubicolo di Veneranda* was painted with intense and brilliant colors in order to remain distinct even in the weak light cast by oil-lamps.

The Appian Way.

THE APPIAN WAY

In the heart of the *archeological park of the Appian Way* is a complex of extraordinary size and surprising beauty, formed by the **Villa**, the **Circus of Maxentius** and the **Mausoleum of Romulus**. Taken together, these architecturally unique buildings are second in importance only to the Imperial palaces of the Palatine. They were built at the beginning of the 4th century by the Emperor Maxentius.

The palace is the less well-preserved of the group; only the apse portions of three rooms, including the *Sala per le Udienze* (Audience Room) are still standing. The **circus**, or the hippodrome, sits in a valley that measures 513 x 91 meters. At the center, the Obelisk of Domitian was recovered, which Bernini later erected on the Fountain of the Four Rivers in Piazza Navona.

The Appian Way continues, with more tombs, beginning with the nearby **Tomb of Cecilia Metella**, a celebrated mausoleum set in an enchanting panorama.

Images from the most important Christian Catacombs. St. Sebastian, St. Callisto and Domitilla.

THE VATICAN CITY

ST. PETER'S BASILICA

In April, 1506, Pope Julius II placed the first stone for the new St. Peter's Basilica, which was to be constructed on the site of the ancient basilica, built in the era of the Emperor Constantine. The task of demolishing the old basilica and the building of the new one was entrusted to Bramante, who worked fervently on the project until his death in 1514. Under Paul V, Maderno adopted definitively the Latin-cross plan.

St. Peter's Square opens to visitors in all its vastness, a sign of the aspiration toward a universal embrace. Bernini designed the piazza, unifying with his architectural genius the most disparate elements, such as the granite *Egyptian obelisk* from the Circus of Nero, which in Roman times occupied the area underneath the piazza and basilica; the *fountain* on the right, designed by Maderno in 1613; and the matching fountain on the left by Carlo Fontana, added in 1677. Bernini himself completed the spectacular elliptical *colonnade*.

The *facade* was realised in 1614 by Carlo Maderno, and like the piazza and the basilica, it has cyclopean dimensions: 48 meters high by 119 meters in width. At the center is the *Loggia delle Benedizioni*, from which the election of every pope is solemnly announced and the pope delivers his benediction "*urbi et orbi*".

In the atrium, above the central door is the *Mosaic of the Navicella*, made by Giotto on the occasion of the Holy Year of 1300. On the opposite wall are five great doors. The 15th-century *Porta Centrale* (Central Door) is dedicated to St. Peter and St. Paul, and was made by Filarete for the old St. Peter's. The other doors were made by contemporary artists. Noteworthy are the *Porta della Morte* (Door of Death) by Giacomo Manzu' (1964) and, at the far right, the **Porta Santa** (Holy Door), opened on the occasion of the Jubilee or Holy Year, which is adorned by scenes of the Old and New Testament by Vico Consorti (1950).

Inside the basilica, one is not immediately crushed by its immensity; instead, an impression of balance prevails, due to the perfect proportion its walls. On the right is the **Cappella della Pieta'** (Chapel of the Pieta') that takes its name from the celebrated marble group that it holds, completed in 1499 by Michelangelo at the age of 24. The intense, expressive beauty and harmonious equilibrium convey the composed dignity of the pain of the Virgin Mary, shown in eternal youth. Also in the right nave is the precious 13th-century *wooden Crucifix* by Pietro Cavallini.

At the end of the central nave are the celebrated remains of the Constantinian building: the *bronze Statue of St. Peter* attributed to Arnolfo di Cambio.

The interior of the Basilica of St. Peter. The center of Bernini's bronze baldacchino.

St. Peter's Square.

The Basilica of St. Peter by night. On the right, the Vatican Palaces.

The **cupola** is an ingenious masterpiece by Michelangelo. This work of arduous engineering rests on the ponderous angular pendentives and set into enormous polygonal pilasters. The immense bronze *baldacchino*, upon which Bernini worked from 1624 to 1633, rises to cover the *papal altar* over the *Tomb of St. Peter* at the level of the Constantinian basilica, which is reached by two stairways which cross the *confessio*.

The *apse* is characterised by the fantastic *Cattedra di San Pietro*, which holds the ancient wooden seat from the first basilica (4th century). Four gigantic figures of the doctors of the church support the Cattedra; above is a luminous round eye with in coloured glass that represents the Holy Spirit in the form of a dove, surrounded by a dynamic vortex of clouds and angels. Bernini worked on the Cattedra between 1657 and 1666, several decades after completing the Baldacchino.

THE ASCENT OF THE DOME

The entrance to the cupola is beyond the right portal of the basilica.

The first portion of the ascent leads to the vast terrace that covers the central nave.

The balustrade, surmounted by gigantic statues of saints, offers a splendid view of St. Peter's Square. Here, the powerful work of Michelangelo seems incumbent upon us: the luminous windows which open on the drum, crowned by matched columns from which plaster ribs depart and run around the Cupola, demonstrate the force and vitality of the sublime artist.

An incredibly vast horizon over the Vatican Gardens and the entire city can be enjoyed from the *lantern* above the cupola, 92 meters above the terrace.

THE VATICAN MUSEUMS

The **Vatican Palaces** are a world unto themselves, at the same time a fantastic and grandiose building of innumerable rooms, salons, museums, galleries, libraries, chapels, courtyards and gardens, rich with countless art treasures of every kind. From the Renaissance on, the great artists left the immortal mark of their genius here. Anyone who loves beautiful things cannot fail to be fascinated by these charming museums.

The entrance to the Vatican Museums in on Viale del Vaticano.

CHIARAMONTI MUSEUM

Founded by Pius VII Chiaramonti (1800-1823), it includes the **Corridor**, the **Lapidary Gallery**, and the **Braccio Nuovo**, all in neoclassical style.

The Corridor, divided into 30 sections, is flanked by two endless rows of statues, busts, sarcophagi and reliefs: about 800 Greco-Roman works; the Lapidary Gallery includes over 5000 pagan and Christian inscriptions. In the Braccio Nuovo, instead, quality is privileged over quantity. Noteworthy is the Statue of Augustus, found in 1863 in the Villa of Livia on the Via Flaminia and brought here by Pope Pius IX.

1) The Biga. A Roman sculpture of the 1st century AD.

2) The Gallery of the Candelabra.

3) The Round Room.

PIO-CLEMENTINE MUSEUM

The museum contains grandiose and munificent works of two popes who lived between the 18th and 19th centuries, Clement XIV and Pius VI, from whom the museum takes its name. The oldest part of it, however, in the Belvedere, dates to Pope Julius II and other popes of the Renaissance.

In the **Sala a Croce Greca** (Greek-Cross Room) there are *two porphyry sarcophogi* which hold the bodies of St. Elena and Constantina, daughter of the Emperor Constantine.

In the **Sala Rotonda** is the magnificent, enormous monolithic *porphyry vase* (4 meters in diameter) from the Domus Aurea, without doubt the richest and most sumptuous object in these galleries. The colossal statue of *Antinoos*, from Palestrina, was ordered by the Emperor Hadrian who deified his young favourite after his premature death.

The **Galleria delle Statue** (Gallery of the Statues) contains interesting works. The *Apollo Sauroctono* is a copy of an exquisite work by Praxiteles; the *Sleeping Arianna* is from the Hellenistic period.

The **Galleria dei Busti** (Gallery of the Busts) follows, which contains Roman-era busts, for the most part. The bust of the young *Augustus* is the real gem of this gallery.

In the **Gabinetto delle Maschere** (Gallery of the Masks) we admire another two treasures of the Vatican collection: the gracious statue of the *Bathing Afrodite*, from an original by Diodalsas of Bitinia, and the famous *Venus of Knido*, perhaps the most beautiful of all the Greek statues, in a world which knew hundreds of masterpieces.

In the **Belvedere Courtyard,** the original Renaissance nucleus of the Museum, the works are placed in four *gabinetti* (rooms), constructed in 1773. The **Gabinetto di Laocoonte** presents a miraculous discovery made among the ruins of the Baths of Titus in 1506: the *Laocoon Group*. The spectacular sculpture was inspired by Virgil's Aeneid. The **Gabinetto dell'Apollo** takes its name from the statue of *Apollo*. The **Gabinetto del Perseo** contains the only modern works on display, placed here when two masterpieces of the museum, *Perseus with the head of Medusa and the Two Pugilists Kreugante and Damosseno*, were taken by Napoleon to Paris; the artist honoured to fill the space was the greatest neoclassical Italian sculptor, Antonio Canova (1757-1822). The **Gabinetto del Mercurio** houses the *Statue of Mercury*, found in 1543 near Castel Sant'Angelo. Pope Paul III had it brought to the Belvedere Gardens. To the left of the Sala Rotonda is the **Gabinetto dell'Apoxyomenos**. In the center rises the *Athlete* by Lysippos (Apoxyomenos), a copy in marble of a Greek original in bronze.

On the right of the Sala Rotonda is the **Atrium of the Torso** (Trunk), with the statue of the Torso at its center, with the name of the sculptor inscribed: "Apollonius, son of Nestor, of Athens, made this" (1st century AD).

The Laocoon. An original Hellenistic work of the 1st century BC.

Right: The vault of the Sistine Chapel, by Michelangelo.

The Belvedere Torso, which dates from 1st century BC.

The Stefaneschi Polyptych by Giotto.

THE RAPHAEL ROOMS
(Le Stanze di Raffaello)

The visit begins in the **Sala di Costantino**, where frescoes include Giulio Romano's *Apparition of the Cross*, which shows Constantine's defeat of Maxentius (312 AD), and the *Baptism of Constantine*, which is on the entry wall. There are also frescoes by Francesco Penni.

The following room is the **Stanza di Eliodoro**, painted in 1511-14, and named for the fresco which portrays the *Castigation of Heliodorus*. Above the window is the scene of the *Miracle at Bolsena*. The *Liberation of St. Peter from prison* was skillfully painted around the window.

In 1508, Pope Julius II commissioned a young Raphael to decorate the four vast rooms of his new residence with large frescoes.

In the next room we admire the first work by Raphael: the *Dispute of the Holy Sacrament*, finished in 1509. On the wall opposite the Dispute is the *School of Athens*; in front, the Exaltation of the faith and the Celebration of reason. Above the window we admire the *Parnassus*, the mythical Greek mountain of the gods.

The last is the **Stanza dell'Incendio del Borgo**, named for the fresco within; on the left wall is the *Naval Victory of Leo IV over the Saracens*.

THE SISTINE CHAPEL

The Sistine Chapel was built by the architect Giovanni de' Dolci between 1475 and 1483 for Pope Sixtus IV, who wanted it to be, from an architectural point of view, as simple as possible -- closed and therefore inaccessible.

In 1508, Julius II, always eager for new projects, ordered the young Michelangelo to paint the **Sistine Ceiling**. The gigantic job, painted over a blue background with golden stars, was begun in May 1508 and finished in 1512. Michelangelo brilliantly overcame the difficulties presented by the enormous size (800 square meters of surface area) and the nudity of the vault. Upon it he superimposed painted architectonic elements into which he arranged the various figures with stunning three-dimensional effect. In the twenty-three years that passed from the time that Michelangelo had finished the decoration of the ceiling until he painted, on the wall of the main altar, the **Last Judgement**, the Christian world was transformed by the Lutheran revolution and Rome suffered the most horrible pillage in its history. The Last Judgment, a compound of Dante's comedy and a visual, exploding

Dies irae was commissioned by Pope Paul III and begun by Michelangelo in 1535. It was completed in 1541.

Three hundred figures crowd the fresco, which is nonetheless stunning for its coherence and clarity, as they are organised into a true architecture of bodies. Christ, implacable judge, dominates the grandiose scene with his right arm raised in condemnation. The Madonna at his side represents the everlasting connection between Christ and humanity.

The Sistine Chapel was the seat of conclaves until the end of the 15th century; its compact and fortified structure rendered it particularly ideal for the secrecy of elective assemblies.

A religious ceremony in the Sistine Chapel with the Pope and cardinals.

VENICE

Venice is a unique city, vibrant with art, culture and history. Its beautiful buildings in the Gothic-Renaissance style, which rise from a labyrinth of tiny islands, canals and bridges, are full of evanescent, mysterious charm.

According to tradition, Venice was founded on March 25th, 421 AD, a date more or less confirmed by history: in the 5th century the inhabitants of the Roman region of "Venetia et Istria" began to move from the mainland to the islands in the lagoon in order to escape the first barbarian invasions, a migration which culminated with the invasion of the Longobards (568). By about 770 the settlers had their own bishop, and 40 years later the political center was transferred to Rivo Alto, modern-day Venice.

By the 10th century, Venice had conquered the coast of Istria and Dalmatia and liberated its waters from pirates. With the Fourth Crusade (1202-1204), Venice penetrated militarily and economically into the entire Mediterranean, becoming the hinge between the Orient and the Western world by virtue of its mercantile traffic. It grew in authority and prestige, extending its possessions through the entire Adriatic basin to the Near East, rivaling Genoa and controlling the territories of the Padania to the west. "Serenissima Repubblica" (The Serene Republic) was the official name of Venice between the middle ages and the Renaissance, when the city was the only great European State which governed itself without monarchs or bishops. The structure of the Republic of Venice was designed from the beginning to prevent power from falling to a single man, so the supreme function assumed by the Doge came under the watchful eyes of different orders of counsellors. They availed themselves of a network of informers who, created a suspicious climate but also granted control of every aspect of city life.

The aristocratic Republic of San Marco thrived on the strength of its civic, military and social institutions, and soon surpassed its rivals - the other maritime republics of Genoa, Pisa and Amalfi. It was above all in the early Renaissance (first half of the 15th century) that Venice reached the height of its power, and the civility of the Republic imposed itself on the world. The Turks were defeated at the battle of Gallipoli in 1416, yielding the Eastern kingdoms of Morea, Cyprus and Candia. In Italy, between 1414 and 1428, the Republic took Verona, Vicenza, and Udine, then Brescia and Bergamo. The Adriatic, as far as Corfu, became the "Venetian Sea," and with Marco Polo's trading, the Venetians reached as far as Asia. But the fall of Constantinople to the Turks in 1453 marked the beginning of Venice's decline. The discovery of America, in addition, changed the direction of the commercial routes from the Mediterranean to the Atlantic. In the 16th century, Venice was forced into an exhausting war against the Turks, which ended only in 1571, with the victory of the Venetians and the Holy League over the Ottomans at the battle of Lepanto. The decay was accentuated in the 17th century, after the Turkish conquest of Candia, following a 25-year siege.

The year 1797 marked the end of the Republic of San Marco. Napoleon conquered the city and abolished a thousand-year-old constitution. He then ceded Venice to Austria by the treaty of Campoformio. Only after long struggles during the Risorgimento (Italian unification movement) and a plebiscite did Venice and the Veneto region become part of a united Italy in 1866.

Venice is an extremely engaging cultural center. Home to Ca'Foscari University; art and cultural institutes, including the very active Fondazione Giorgio Cini; several theatres, among them the Fenice, recently destroyed by a devastating fire and currently being rebuilt; numerous museums of great importance, including Palazzo Ducale, the Correr, the Museum of the 18th Century, the Accademia Gallery, the Modern Art Gallery, the Guggenheim Collection and the Museum of Maritime History.

The Venetian Lagoon is separated from the sea by a sand-bank known as the Lido. Once frequented by the Viennese court of the Archduke Maximilian of Austria, it was developed above all between the First and Second World Wars. Today, the Lido is famous for its beaches, luxury hotels, casino and the International Film Festival, inaugurated on the Lido in 1932.

Like the Lido, the various islands that face Venice -- Giudecca, Murano, Burano and Torcello -- are easily reached by vaporetto (water bus), which, together with the characteristic gondolas and motorboats, represent the most common mode of transportation in the lagoon.

A magnificent ceremony has taken place in Venice since 1000 AD on Assumption Day, as a re-evocation of the conquest of the coastal cities of Istria and Dalmatia: the "Sposalizio del Mare" (the Wedding with the Sea). From the boat Il Bucintoro, the Doge throws a ring into the sea and says: "Ti sposiamo, o mare nostro, in segno di vero e perpetuo dominio" (We marry you, our sea, as a sign of true and eternal dominance).

One of the oldest and most glorious celebrations in Venice is the famous Regata Storica (Historical Regatta) on the first Sunday in September. Every year since 1300, crowds of Venetians and tourists have gathered along the Grand Canal, which is festooned in banners and damask for the event. After the procession of the picturesque flotilla of the "bissone" (sumptuous boats conducted by gondoliers in 15th-century costume) comes the race of the "gondolini". More than a simple athletic competition, the Regata Storica is a popular celebration in which the true protagonist is the gondola, symbol of the soul and tradition of Venice.

LIST OF THE MONUMENTS

1) St. Mark's Square.
2) The Basilica of St. Mark.
3) The Piazzetta.
4) The Marciana Library.
5) Doge's Palace.
6) The Bridge of Sighs.
7) Santa Maria della Salute.
8) Palazzo Grassi.

9) Palazzo Mocenigo.
10) Rialto Bridge.
11) Fondaco dei Tedeschi.
12) Ca' d'Oro.
13) Palazzo Vendramin Calergi.
14) Palazzo Labia.
15) Ponte degli Scalzi.
16) Ca' Pesaro.

17) Palazzo Bernardo.
18) Ca' Foscari.
19) Ca' Rezzonico.
20) Accademia Bridge.
21) The Church of the Frari.
22) Accademia Galleries.

PIAZZA SAN MARCO

The piazza, universally known as the most beautiful "*salon of the world*," offers the visitor a unique scene. Dominated by the facade of the Basilica di San Marco, harmoniously inserted between the Torre dell'Orologio and the Campanile, St. Mark's Square is closed on three sides by almost half a kilometer of porticoes. On the side of the Mercerie are those called "*Procuratie Nuove*", and on the side of the bell tower are those called "*Procuratie Vecchie*", which host the *Caffe' Florian*, one of the oldest coffee parlours in the city. At the far end, opposite the basilica, the Ala Napoleonica holds the **Museo Correr**. It contains part of the collection of the Venetian Teodoro Correr, including splendid works by Antonio Canova, a collection of paintings by artists such as Antonello da Messina, Vittore Carpaccio, Giovanni Bellini, and some antique pieces that date to the time of the Republic.

Over the course of centuries, St. Mark's Square was the stage upon which the major historical, political and cultural events in Venice played out. It reached its greatest splendour when the Republic, with the intention to exalt the greatness and power the city had reached, approved a project of architectural restoration and urbanisation which had as its first objective the restructuring of the piazza. The work began in 1529 and went on for more than 30 years under the direction of Jacopo Sansovino. This commission turned the young architect into a real interpreter of the State's architectural plans. The piazza was enlarged, the **Procuratie Vecchie** were completed, the *Basilica* and *Campanile* were restored, and the construction of the **Biblioteca Marciana** (Marciana Library) on the Piazzetta, which remains one of the most important works of Sansovino, was begun.

Sansovino's successor, the architect Scamozzi, completed the Libreria and built the **Procuratie Nuove** in place of the Orseolo hospice, which had to be pulled down because it was too old and unattractive to stand with the other buildings. The piazza, which at the beginning of the 18th century was paved in red-bricks in a herring-bone pattern, was repaved in 1723 with slabs of gray stone outlined with strips of Istria stone. At the center, in front of the portal of the Basilica di San Marco, rise three tall ship masts, the so-called "Pili" that stand on three basements. On festival days, the flag of San Marco is raised.

St. Mark's Square, with the Basilica and Campanile.

The Basin of San Marco, with the Basilica di Santa Maria della Salute in the background.

The Campanile di San Marco and the Doge's Palace.

The interior of the Basilica of St. Mark.

Detail of a mosaic in the Basilica.

BASILICA DI SAN MARCO

On Piazza San Marco, set in a splendid architectural scene between the Torre dell'Orologio and the Campanile di San Marco, is the Basilica di San Marco, which has been the cathedral of the city since 1807. Its origins go back to 832, when St. Mark the Evangelist replaced San Teodoro as the city's patron saint. St. Mark's remains, which two merchants stole from the Maomettans of Alexandria, were brought to Venice in the year 828 and temporarily interred in a chapel inside Palazzo Ducale. When it was felt that the holy relics deserved to be held in a real church, a church-mausoleum was built in 832. Following a civil revolt in 976, the Doge's Palace, the traditional seat of power, was set on fire and the nearby church was destroyed. Pietro Orseolo, the saint, had the church rebuilt over the following two years, and in 978 the sanctuary was consecrated.

In 1063, the city of Venice, by then rich and powerful, felt the need to express its progress and growth, above all in architecture. In this period of enormous development, the Basilica of San Marco was again rebuilt, following a pure Byzantine model, with the central plan in the form of a Greek cross, surmounted by a bulbed dome and four cupolas of unequal height on the four arms.

Between the 11th and 15th centuries, the basilica underwent remarkable modifications and changes, above all in the ornamentation of the facade, which today features two levels with five arches, of which the central ones are the largest. The five doorways on the first level, which juts out slightly, are separated by a double row of precious multicolored marble columns. Each doorway is covered in fine reliefs of biblical scenes, the various the "Mestieri" (principal businesses in Venice) and the signs of the zodiac. The lunettes above the *doorways* feature Byzantine-style *mosaic decoration* with a background of gold. The large central lunette represents the Last Judgement; those on the sides the essential moments of the transportation of the body of St. Mark; and the last on the left, which is the oldest (13th century), shows the basilica as it was before the addition of the Gothic elements.

The upper central arch is closed by a window that brings light to the interior and serves as a background for the *famous bronze horses*. The other upper lunettes, also in mosaic on gold, feature the *Deposition*, the *Descent into Limbo*, the *Resurrection* and the *Ascension*. The view is completed by the five domes which culminate in oil lamps and crosses in the Oriental style.

The basilica is entered through an atrium paved in marble and mosaic (13th-century). The central presbytery, separated from the lateral naves by columns with capitals which support architraves, is decorated with Gothic statues (14th-century). At the end, behind the main altar, glitters the famous *Pala d'oro* (Golden Altarpiece), one of

The Basilica of San Marco.

the most precious works in gold in the world. Ordered from Constantinople by the Doge Pietro Orseolo (976-978), it was subsequently enriched and reassembled. In 1345, a goldsmith from Siena, Gian Paolo Buoninsegna, created the Pala as we see it today for the Doge Andrea Dandolo.

The *urn* with the *remains of St. Mark* is under the main altar, which is surmounted by a *baldacchino* supported by four green marble columns, sculpted with biblical scenes. There are several noteworthy chapels: the *chapel dedicated to the Madonna Nicopeia*, who is considered the protector of Venice, is the most venerated image in the

Basilica; and the *Chapel of San Clemente*, from which the Doge attended mass unseen, sitting behind an iron grate to the right of the altar.

Also worth admiring is the **Baptistery**, with Sansovino's baptismal font (1545). The 14th-century mosaics which decorate the walls feature scenes from the life of Christ, in which the Crucifixion makes up the background of the main altar, and *scenes from the life of St. John the Evangelist*.

It is worth noting that the image of *Salome' dancing with the head of St. John the Baptist, obtained from King Herod for her performance*, is still a work of great expres-

The Basilica of San Marco. Detail of the facade.

sive reality. Next to the baptistery, the *Zen Chapel* is decorated by 14th-century mosaics which tell the story of the life of St. Mark.

The 4000 square meters of surface area that over the centuries were covered with mosaics render the basilica unlike any other in the world for its splendour and magnificence. The intention to illustrate the sacred story of the Bible to the faithful is easily grasped when observing the images of the first prophets, the apostles and the Ascension and Paradise in the great domes.

The mosaic above the main doorway of the Basilica.

THE PIAZZETTA

The piazzetta lies where in the early days of the Republic there was nothing more than a dock where the rio (canal) Batario came in as far as the edge of the wall of the **Torre del Campanile**. In the 12th century , the rio was filled in and part of the dock was replaced by the small square.

Inserted between the **Palazzo Ducale** and the **Libreria Sansoviniana** (Sansovinian Library), the enchanting piazzetta seems almost a connection between San Marco and the lagoon. The two columns in oriental granite which stand near the lagoon were brought in the 12th century from Constantinople and mark the official entrance to the city, which at the time was reachable only by sea. The space between the two columns was considered a "zona franca" (free-trade area) and a place where gambling was allowed. The columns are called of *Marco* and of *Todaro*, in reference to the symbols posed atop each one. In fact, above the one closer to the Libreria Marciana is the statue of the first patron of the city of Venice, the *Greek warrior Theodor* (in Venetian dialect Todaro); from above the other column, the omnipresent *winged lion* of Venice dominates.

The Piazzetta San Marco.

47

Aerial view of the Doge's Palace.

Balcony of the Sala del Maggior Consiglio.

DOGE'S PALACE

The *Palazzo Ducale*, or *Doge's Palace*, dominates the piazzetta and the bank of the Basin of San Marco; in its splendour, it is a refined example of the Venetian-Gothic style. It began to take form in the first half of the 14th century, passing through three phases of construction, followed by illustrious artists and architects of the period. The building, once home to the Doge and official seat of the government and cultural associations, preserves its original appearance, with two principal facades, each with three levels: a *portico* with pointed arches supported by 36 columns, a *loggia* with two arches for every arch below, a *wall* decorated in white, gray and red marble diamonds with pointed windows and quatrefoil roundels. The profile of the walls is decorated by a Venetian-Byzantine marble crenelation.

From the 15th-century *Porta della Carta* (1438), named for the decrees which were once posted there, one passes through the Foscari portico in the interior courtyard, with Gothic-Renaissance tracts and Baroque elements (clock facade by Monopola (1615). The *Scala dei Giganti* (Stairway of the Giants), designed by Antonio Rizzo in 1485, with the enormous *statues* by Sansovino of *Neptune* and *Mars* that stand above it, leads to the loggiato on the first floor that goes along three sides of the courtyard and the two external facades. At the top of the stairs, on the right, is the *Sala della Cancelleria Inferiore* (Room of the Lower Chancelry) and the *Stanza dei Provveditori alla Milizia del Mar* from which the naval armada was once directed. The *First* and *Second Sale dell'Avogaria* follow, where lawyers worked. From the second room one could reach the *Palazzo delle Prigioni*, by way of a corridor which led to the Bridge of Sighs. The 16th century *Scala d'Oro* leads from the gallery on the first floor to the upper floors (also called noble floors), and connects the main loggia with the numerous rooms above. Culminating in a square atrium with a golden ceiling and paintings by Tintoretto, the stairway leads to the right to the *Sala della Quattro Porte* (antechamber), then to the *Sala dell'Anticollegio*, a sort of waiting room with Veronese's Kidnapping of Europa and mythological paintings by Tintoretto; and finally to the *Sala del Collegio*, where the Doge discussed affairs of State with his counsellors.

The ceiling is decorated with paintings by Veronese, while the walls feature portraits of Doges by Tintoretto. From the Sala delle Quattro Porte, one passes to the *Sala del Consiglio dei Dieci*, which contains a splendid coffered ceiling with panels painted by Veronese. After crossing the *Sala della Bussola* (Room of the Compass) the *Sale d'Armi* (Armory) and the *Sala dei Tre Capi del Consiglio dei Dieci* (Room of the Three Heads of the Council of Ten) one reaches the most beautiful room in the Palace, the *Sala del Maggior Consiglio* (seat of the governing body). Here, the walls recount the history of Venice with paintings by various masters; above the Doge's throne, resting against the far wall, is Tintoretto's *Paradise*, one of the largest paintings in the world.

The Sala del Senato.

Palazzo Ducale and Piazzetta San Marco at night.

The Bell Tower of St. Mark.

THE CAMPANILE DI SAN MARCO

The campanile (bell tower) that holds the bells of San Marco, rises at the point where St. Mark's Square and the Piazzeta meet. Built in the 9th century as a watchtower over the dock, which at the time began where the Piazzetta is now, the campanile underwent notable changes as a result of the various types of damage it suffered over the centuries that followed.

Sadly, on the morning of July 14th, 1902, the campanile collapsed. No one was hurt, nor was the basilica damaged, but the Loggetta del Sansovino (below) was destroyed. It was decided to rebuild it "*dov'era e com'era*" (where it was and how it was) using the original materials where possible.

The 99-meter tall tower offers a beautiful panorama of the city and the lagoon. The belfry contains five bells and is surmounted by a drum, which is covered by a pyramid shaped cusp and topped by a golden statue of the Archangel Gabriel, which moves with the wind.

THE TORRE DELL'OROLOGIO

The Clock Tower, seen from the Basilica of St. Mark.

On the northern side of the Piazza is the Torre dell'Orologio, built during the Renaissance (1496-1499), whose monumental doorways allowed passage to the *Mercerie*, the most important commercial street in Venice. The central portion, which is the most interesting part of the whole building, remains in original condition. Above the arcade of the door is the famous *orologio* (clock), studded with golden stars against a background of blue enamel. The decoration is completed by the signs of the zodiac and the planets in relief. In a niche above the great clock is a sculpture of the *Madonna and Child*, in gilded copper. To the sides of the niche are the hours in Roman numerals and the minutes in Arabic numerals.

Looking further up, one admires the *Winged Lion*, symbol of St. Mark, which stands out against a blue background filled with stars.

At the top of the tower, two statues in bronze, nicknamed "I Mori" (the Moors) for their color, are connected to a sophisticated internal mechanism that announces the hours by ringing the large central bell.

According to legend, after building the tower, the brothers Paolo and Carlo Ranieri were struck blind by the Venetians to ensure that they could not build anything as beautiful or perfect.

THE BRIDGE OF SIGHS

The so-called "Pozzi" or "Piombi", the state prisons in the Palazzo Ducale, became unusable because of overcrowding and the poor condition of the prisoners. It was therefore decided that a new prison be built in an adjacent building beyond the rio di Palazzo. The new prisons were finished in 1610, but the connecting bridge had been completed eight years earlier. This sadly famous small bridge, declaimed by writers in the 19th century, was given the nickname "Bridge of Sighs" to underline the grave and heavy-hearted route that the prisoners had to walk. After sentencing, they returned to their cells to serve the penalty that had been imposed. Only from the two perforated marble windows of the bridge could they have one final glance at the lagoon, before going to their hole-like place of confinement.

Architecturally, the bridge is distinguished for the height at which it is placed and its closed sides. Internally, it is composed of two corridors divided by a wall; one leads to the rooms of the Tribunale, the other to the rooms of the Avogaria. A secondary stairway also connects it to the Pozzi or Piombi.

The Bridge of Sighs on the Rio di Palazzo.

SANTA MARIA DELLA SALUTE

The basilica is on the point of the Dogana (Customs office) and faces the Basin of San Marco. Built in gratitude to the Virgin Mary for having brought the terrible plague of 1630 to an end, it was commissioned in 1631 from a young architect, Baldassare Longhena. It is undoubtedly a great testimony to Venetian Baroque architecture.

Constructed on an octagonal plan and rich in ornamental statues, the basilica culminates with two hemispherical domes, one smaller and with two slender bell towers in the rear. The central *facade* has the aspect of a Triumphal Arch; the six lateral facades correspond to the six chapels which line the inside of the basilica. Above the entrance tympanum is a *Statue of the Madonna and Child* to signify the glorification of Mary. *Inside*, one admires the central space, paved by a beautiful mosaic of concentric circles in polychromatic marble, surrounded by a band of 32 roses which symbolize the Rosary of Mary. The *altar*, also octagonal, shows the plague fleeing from the Madonna in the marble statue that adorns it.

The *sacristy* contains precious canvases by Titian, such as *St. Mark Enthroned with the Saints* and *The Sacrifice of Isaac, David and Goliath, Cain and Abel*, as well as the *Wedding of Cana* that Tintoretto painted in 1561.

CANAL GRANDE

The spectacle that can be enjoyed, gliding along the Grand Canal, transported by the slow rhythm of a gondola and immersed in the silence offered by the city on the lagoon, cannot be compared to anything else.

Still the main traffic conduit for Venetians, this wide canal elegantly winds across town for about four kilometers, tracing an inverted "S" and dividing Venice into two parts. The uninterrupted and harmonious series of churches, prestigious palaces and refined buildings with splendid decorations brings an immense joy to the observant eye.

The Grand Canal, from which 45 rii (small canals) depart, is traversed by three bridges: the *Rialto Bridge* (see below); the *Scalzi Bridge*, which was built in iron at the beginning of the 19th century and later rebuilt in stone by Eugenio Miozzi in 1934; and the *Accademia Bridge*, still made of wood (a 1933 plan to rebuild it in stone was never realised). Leaving from the Punta della Dogana da Mar and following the right bank, among the first palaces is the *Contarini Fasan*, also called the "dimora di Desdemona" (Desdemona's residence), in late-15th century Florentine-Gothic style, followed by *Palazzo Ferri-Fini* and the celebrated Hotel *Pisani-Gritti*, where Hemingway stayed. Next

Ca' Pesaro.

Palazzo Cavalli Franchetti.

Ca' Foscari.

is the majestic *Palazzo Corner della Ca' Grande*, designed for a noble family by Sansovino; today the palace is home to the Prefeture of Venice. The *Casetta delle Rose*, where D'Annunzio stayed during the First World War, is followed by *Palazzo Barbaro* and *Palazzo Cavalli Franchetti*. The 17th-century *Palazzo Giustinian Lolin*, by Longhena and once the residence of the Duchess of Parma, is today the seat of the music center of the Levi Foundation. Next is the late-18th century *Palazzo Grassi* by Giorgio Massari, which today houses prestigious art expositions. *Palazzo Contarini delle Figure* (of the Figures) takes its name from the caryatids which support the balcony. *Palazzo Mocenigo Vecchio* follows, which belonged to an important Venetian family who gave the city seven doges. Then come *Palazzo Mocenigo Nuovo*, the Gothic *Palazzo Garzoni*, and the *Renaissance Palazzo Corner Spinelli*. Palazzo Benzon, rebuilt in the 18th century, was an important meeting point for writers and nobles, such as Foscolo, Canova and Lord Byron. The imposing *Palazzo Grimani* (16th-century) is today the seat of the Court of Appeals and the two 13th-century palaces, *Ca' Farsetti* and *Ca' Loredan*, currently hold city offices.

After the Rialto Bridge rises the *Fondaco dei Tedeschi*, once a warehouse for German merchants and today seat of the central Post Office. Next follow *Ca' Da Mosto*, one of the oldest 13th-century Venetian houses, later transformed into the famous hotel "Del Leon Bianco", and *Palazzo Michiel dalle Colonne* (the name alludes to the columns on which the upper floors rest). Up ahead is the most beautiful palace of this side of the canal, the famous **Ca d'Oro**, an excellent example, along with Palazzo Ducale, of the ornate Venetian-Gothic. Rich in precious goldwork which once adorned the facade, in 1927 it became the seat of the **Museo Franchetti**, and later was donated, along with the collection, to the State. Along the way are palaces well-worth admiring: *Palazzo Gussoni-Grimani*, whose facade was once adorned by frescoes by Tintoretto, *Palazzo Vendramin Calergi*, today home to the Casino in winter,

The Ca' d'Oro on the Canal Grande.

Palazzo Correr-Contarini; *Palazzo Labia*, now seat of the RAI (Italian state radio and television), with precious frescoes by Tiepolo; and, before the Ponte degli Scalzi, there is *Palazzo Calbo Crotta*, one of the first palaces on the Grand Canal, which became the Hotel Principe.

Returning along the other side of the Canal, after the *Church of San Simeon Piccolo* (18th century), we first see *Palazzo Foscari-Contarini*, the *Fondaco dei Turchi*, which in 1621 was the warehouse of the Turkish merchants in Venice. Following are *Palazzo Belloni Battaglia*, commissioned from Baldassare Longhena by the rich merchant, Girolamo Belloni, and *Palazzo Tron*.

After the *Church of San Stae* and the *Church of Sant'Eustachio*, which probably dates to before the 11th century, is *Ca' Pesaro*, another work by Longhena and seat of the *Museo d'Arte Orientale* and the *Museo d'Arte Moderna*. *Ca' Corner della Regina* is where Caterina Cornaro, the queen of Cyprus, was born in 1454.

After passing the *Fabbriche Nuove* and the *Fabbriche Vecchie*, two long buildings which in the past held offices of the administration and authorities, one reaches the *Palazzo dei Camerlenghi* and then, crossing the *Rialto Bridge*, the mid-16th century *Palazzo Papadopoli*, and the elegant *Palazzo Bernardo*. *Palazzo Barbarigo della Terrazza*, named for its enormous and splendid terrace, precedes *Palazzo Pisani-Moretta*, which still preserves its interior decorations, and *Palazzo Balbi*, today seat of the Veneto Regional Council. Opposite is *Ca' Foscari*, a Gothic palace commissioned by the Doge Francesco Foscari, and further down *Palazzo Giustinian*. Next follows Longhena's *Ca' Rezzonico* and *Palazzo Loredan*, named "Degli Ambasciatori" because it was the seat of the Ambassador of Austria.

After *Palazzo Contarini degli Scrigni* and the *Accademia Bridge*, we see palazzi which are worthy of careful observation, like the *Contarini-Polignac*, the *Balbi Valier* and the *Palazzo da Mola*. *Palazzo Dario*, rich in polychromatic marble, along with the *Abbazia di San Gregorio* (15th-century) lead back to the Basilica of Santa Maria della Salute and to the Dogana da Mar.

San Giorgio by Andrea Mantegna.

MUSEUM OF THE VENETIAN 18th CENTURY

The numerous rooms of the **Palazzo Rezzonico**, reconstructed based on a model of an 18th-century Venetian patrician palace, house this museum with diverse works of art, paintings, frescoes, statues, ancient costumes, a puppet theatre, a pharmacy and a gondola.

Among the most valuable paintings are frescoes by Giambattista Tiepolo (the *Wedding of Ludovico Rezzonico*, the *Allegory of Merit between Nobility and Virtue*, the *Strength and Wisdom*) , works by Francesco and Antonio Guardi, pastels by Rosalba Carriera and pictures with subjects of Venetian life by Pietro Longhi.

In addition, there are also the *Camera dei Pagliacci* (Room of the Clowns), the *Camerino degli stucchi* (Room of the Stuccoes), the *Chiesetta* (little church) frescoed by Tiepolo in 1749 and the *Sala del Ridotto* (Meeting Room) to admire.

ACCADEMIA GALLERY

The *Gallerie dell'Accademia* are in the ex-School of Santa Maria della Carita', where they have been since 1807 with the name *Accademia delle Belle Arti* (Academy of the Arts). In 1817, a picture gallery open to the public was installed with an exposition of works, some donated by 18th-century artists and others which belonged to the Republic. This original nucleus was later enlarged and enriched by private donations, as well as treasuries of convents and churches suppressed by Napoleon and obviously, in recent times, by acquisitions made by the State.

The rooms therefore contain a complete panorama of Venetian painting from its origins to the 18th century. In the first room are works by Paolo and Lorenzo Veneziano, considered the best artists of the 14th century, along with Jacobello del Fiore. Among the notable works of the 15th century are those by the Bellini brothers, to whom the Gallery devotes several rooms, in which it is possible to admire the *Madonna and Child between St. Catherine and the Magdalene*, the *Miracle of the Cross fallen in the Canal of San Lorenzo*, and the two altar-pieces *San Giobbe* and *San Zaccaria*. Other remarkable works of the 15th century include the *Legend of St. Ursula* by Vittore Carpaccio.

Among the painters of the 16th century, Giorgione stands out as one of the most innovative for the particularly luminous quality of his paintings. The subject of *The Tempest*, his most important work, is nature exalted in its harmonious relation with man. Also representing the 16th century are Titian's *St. John the Baptist* and *Pieta'*, which the artist had begun painting for his own tomb, finished after his death by his follower Palma il Giovane.In addition, the *Miracle of St. Mark and Adam and Eve* by Tintoretto, Paolo Veronese's masterpiece of a Venetian banquet-scene, *Christ in the House of Levi*, are quite notable. The gallery also contains 17th-century works by minor artists such as Strozzi, Maffei and Mazzone. Among the painters of the 18th century, Canaletto, Tiepolo and Rosalba Carriera stand out.

The Miracle of the Slave, by Tintoretto.

The Tempest by Giorgione.

The Rialto Bridge on the Grand Canal.

RIALTO BRIDGE

Initially built in wood, the bridge was the first and only connection between the banks of the Grand Canal until the 19th century. The first construction was burned during an insurrection in 1310; the second collapsed under an excess of weight in 1444; the third, a true work of carpentry which had a moving part in the center to allow the passage of large ships with heavy cargo, was restored several times before it too collapsed. In 1557, the local government decided to build a more stable bridge out of stone. The economic and architectural difficulties were great, but in 1588, the project of Antonio da Ponte prevailed over those of other illustrious names, such as Michelangelo, Palladio, Vignola and Sansovino, who had all participated in the competition. Da Ponte's design called for a length of 28 meters and a single arch seven meters above the water, so as to allow for the passage of the "galere" (galleys). The work was finished in 1591; the two rows of shops, which today constitute a great tourist attraction, are a later addition.

BASILICA DEI FRARI

The Church of Santa Maria Gloriosa dei Frari was built by Franciscan friars around 1250 near an ancient Benedictine abbey, donated to them by the State. At the beginning of the 15th century, the church was demolished to make way for the present basilica, built in the Romanesque-Gothic style with red brick and white Istria stone.

In its sobriety, the Church of the Frari is the Venice's largest architectural complex, as well as the richest in works of art, after that of the Basilica of San Marco. Called the *Pantheon* of the city for its many illustrious tombs, the Franciscan complex is made up of the church, the campanile, and the ancient convent of the Frari, today home to the State Archives. The *facade* of the church is divided in three parts by pilasters surmounted by tiny shrines in the Venetian-Byzantine style, and features a pointed arch upon which there are statues of *Christ*, *St. Francis* and the *Virgin*.

The *interior*, with a Latin-cross plan, has three naves marked by 12 pilasters which sustain very high pointed arches. In the central nave, one can admire the ancient Coro dei Frari (Choir stalls). Made up of 124 precious seats in inlaid wood, the well-preserved work by the Cozzi family of Vicenza is a true rarity.

In the right nave is the *Tomb of Titian*, who died in the plague of 1576, made by the followers of Canova.

The interior of the Church of the Frari.

Rio San Barnaba.

VENICE'S CARNEVALE

Venetian Carnevale (Carnival) has very remote origins. The use of masks was already diffuse in the 14th century, so much so that the local "mask makers" had their own guild. In the time of the Republic, the Carnevale celebrations began on December 26th and finished on the Thursday before Lent when, in the courtyards of every nobel palace, various spectacles took place, among them the rite of the killing of the animals by the head of the butcher's guild. During this period, one could transgress social rules, the Republic became more tolerant toward all citizens and the masks functioned as a means to change identity and temporarily hide social differences. Concerts and dances were held in the larger campi (squares), on St. Mark's Square and on the Piazzetta.

Over the years, Carnevale in Venice has acquired an ever-growing fame, attracting thousands of visitors to the annual celebration. In the period that precedes Lent, the city is transformed into an immense stage, with thousands of multi-coloured costumed performers on parade.

The ancient traditions have not vanished. Dances, performances and games are still organised as they once were. On the last day of Carnevale, the traditional *rogo della Vecchia* takes place, in which the effigy of Carnevale in the shape of an old woman made of straw is burned in Piazza San Marco as a propitious rite of renewal.

The masquerade of Venice's famous Carnevale.

MURANO

Navigating across the canals, which constitute a true submerged road network, one reaches Murano. The largest "island" in the lagoon is formed by five tiny islands, about 1.5 km from Venice.

Murano was once an important commercial center based on salt production and fishing. The population soon grew excessive, so much so that in the 9th century, the concerned Doge invited some inhabitants to move to Venice.

Governed by its own set of laws, the island elected its own Maggior Consiglio (group of leaders) until 1797. Murano owes its fame to glasswork. At the end of the 13th century, in fact, the Venetian glassworks were transferred to Murano for security reasons (glassworks were considered a dangerous source of fires).

Illustrious families of artisans such as the Barovier, Toso and Ballarin concentrated their efforts on the search for materials and working techniques; the results obtained over the years rendered Venetian glass famous in all the world, a reputation that continues today.

With the increase in population and the necessity of creating new residential zones, the ancient sumptuousness of the island slipped away little by little; yet, aside from the busy glass workshops, it is still possible to admire interesting buildings, like the **Duomo of Sts. Mary and Donato**, one of the oldest churches in the lagoon, rich with precious medieval mosaics which decorate its pavement and walls.

Typical view of Burano.

BURANO

Upon reaching the island of Burano, about 9 km. from Venice, one can distinguish the bright colors of the houses, which lack the ornamentation of the palaces of the rest of Veneto region, and confer a pleasant and cheerful air to the island. Nicknamed the "*Island of Lace*", Burano began to develop this feminine handicraft around the 16th century; after a long period of glory, it reached a level of refined virtuosity at the end of the 18th century. The novelty that the lace-makers of the island brought to this art consisted of the so-called "punto in aria" (stitch in the air) – lace worked with the needle – which became the specialty of Burano.

The success that Burano lace-makers enjoyed over the years, with ever more requests for their work from many noble families and the haute bourgeoisie of Europe, necessitated a large-scale production, and therefore the creation of a special school for lace-making on the island. Unfortunately, around the 18th century, due to the advent of foreign competition (above all French), not to mention the decay of the Venetian Republic, this thriving business lost its fame and almost disappeared.

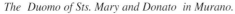

The Duomo of Sts. Mary and Donato in Murano.

FLORENCE

A city in which the Italian genius manifests itself with the greatest brilliance and intensity, Florence is world famous for its cultural and artistic traditions. Capital of the region of Tuscany, itself worthy of a thorough visit for its natural beauty and the splendors of its towns, Florence rises in a shell surrounded by gentle hills in the middle basin of the Arno river. It was founded by the Romans as Florentia in 59BC on the right bank of the Arno, right where the Ponte Vecchio now stands, and it very early became a prosperous commercial center. After a dark period of domination by the Byzantines and Longobards, the city was restored to dignity by the Carolingian dynasty.

In 1078, at the time of the battle for investiture, Florence took the side of the Countess Matilda di Canossa, who gave the town its autonomy. Over the course of the 12th century, the city prospered under the influence of the new merchant class. The crafts were organised into powerful Corporations for the Arts and Crafts; in those years the Guilds of Silk and Wool employed a third of the population and exported products in Europe with the financial help of Florentine bankers. From 1215, Florentine political life was dominated by the conflict between two noble factions: the Guelfs, sustainers of the Pope; and the Ghibellines, who supported the Holy Roman Emperor.

This battle continued, among other events, for many years. Even Dante, a Guelf supporter, participated in the battle of Campaldino (1289) and in 1302 these antagonisms led to his permanent exile from Florence. The terrible plague of 1348 decimated the Florentine population, and brought an end to this rivalry.

For more than three hundred years (from the 12th to the 15th centuries), Florence was the cradle of creative spirits of every sort: from the immense poet Dante, to Cimabue, Giotto, Botticelli, Brunelleschi, Donatello and through to Michelangelo, a man of the highest art and thought.

Florence became a constitutional signoria in 1434 under Cosimo de' Medici, who wisely ruled over the city for thirty years. He pursued a policy of equilibrium between the Italian states, which was also followed by his grandson Lorenzo il Magnifico (the Magnificent) (1469-1492), under whom the arts and letters prospered.

In this period, Humanism developed in Italy, and with it the Renaissance. Even if associated with battles, crises between towns, wars between city-states and foreign invasions, in Florence these movements were at the same time synonymous with intellectual and spiritual beauty. They generated entirely new ideas and became the driving force behind the illustrious men of the period.

As a result, painting, sculpture and architecture, as well as music, literature and all the arts underwent a stunning transformation that had the effect of a real "revolution." Artists from the period include Paolo Uccello, Beato Angelico, Sandro Botticelli, Pollaiolo and Ghirlandaio as well as Leon Battista Alberti, Filippo Brunelleschi and Benvenuto Cellini.

In the 16th century, the second Renaissance, which was centred in Rome, developed in Florence. Leonardo, Michelangelo and Raphael did their artistic apprenticeships in Florence and later created works which inspired the so-called mannerism, a term which refers to their cold, rational and highly intellectual style.

The Medici family ruled Florence and the yet to be born Grand duchy of Tuscany until the 18th century, with several interruptions. The last prestigious Medici, Ferdinand I, married a French Princess, Christina of Lorraine. From then on, the Austrian house of Lorraine ruled Florence (with the exception of a decade under Napoleon at the beginning of the 19th century) with great liberalism and cultural openness, until the city was annexed into the State of Italy in 1860.

The city suffered considerably during the Second World War, and was gravely damaged in the terrible flood of November, 1966. In recent years, Florence has again become magnificent, thanks to the strong commitment of the citizens and to the help which came from near and far. Today, along with Rome and Venice, it is one of the most loved cities in Italy, visited by tourists from all over the world.

In the course of a brief visit it is impossible to see all that the city offers. It is much better to choose according to personal taste that which is most interesting, and leave the rest, because even in an extremely short amount of time Florence manages to reveal its fascinating essence to the visitor. In any case, its monuments, museums and works of art are generally just a short, pleasant walk away from Piazza della Signoria.

One must not speak of Florence without mentioning Tuscany and its terrain, such as Chianti and Mugello, the medieval cities of Siena, Lucca, Pisa, Pistoia and towns like Pienza and San Gimignano.

The image of the region immediately reminds us of the landscapes in the works of Duccio di Buoninsegna, Pietro Lorenzetti, Bartolo di Fredi or Sano di Pietro: a gently sloping, fertile countryside covered in vineyards and studded with old houses, farms and sparse villas. The numerous abbeys, country residences and manor houses perched on the most attractive hills, along with the many castles which testify to century-old battles for control of the land, are all that remain from the time when the fields were managed according to the share cropping system.

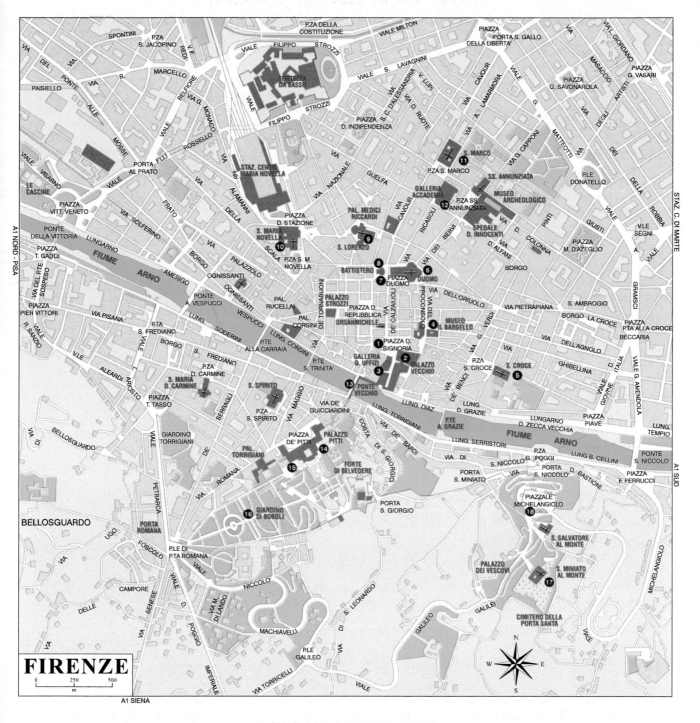

LIST OF THE MONUMENTS

1) Piazza della Signoria.
2) Palazzo Vecchio.
3) The Uffizi Gallery.
4) Palace and National Museum of Bargello.
5) The Basilioca of Santa Croce.
6) The Duomo.
7) Campanile di Giotto.
8) Battistero di San Giovanni.
9) San Lorenzo.
10) Santa Maria Novella.
11) The Church of St. Mark.
12) Accademia Gallery.
13) Ponte Vecchio.
14) Pitti Palace.
15) Galleria Palatina.
16) The Boboli Gardens.
17) San Miniato al Monte.
18) Piazzale Michelangelo.

PIAZZA DELLA SIGNORIA

For many centuries, Piazza della Signoria was at the heart of the city's historical and political events. It is dominated by the 13th-century *Palazzo Vecchio* (or *Palazzo della Signoria*) on its northern side and by the late-Gothic *Loggia dei Lanzi*, built by Benci di Cione and Simone Talenti (1376-82), to the right of the facade. The Loggia dei Lanzi, named after the Lanzichenecchi (Cosimo I's bodyguards), today holds various sculptures, including the *Rape of the Sabine* and *Hercules and the Centaur*, both by Giambologna, and Cellini's *Perseus*.

Other sculptures in the Piazza della Signoria are: the 16th-century *Fountain of Neptune* by Bartolomeo Ammannati, which represents the God of the Sea standing in a chariot pulled by sea horses (the statue is nicknamed "biancone" or "big white guy" for its color and large size); the *Equestrian Monument of Cosimo I* (1594) by Giambologna; a copy of Michelangelo's *David* (the original is in the Galleria dell'Accademia); the group of *Hercules and Cacus* by Bandinelli, and the Donatello-like *bronze* representing *Judith and Holofernes*.

PALAZZO VECCHIO

The Palazzo Vecchio or *Palazzo della Signoria* is an imposing Gothic palace built in rusticated pietra forte by Arnolfo di Cambio in 1294. Its summit finishes with a crenelation surmounted by an elegant *Tower* (1310), 94 meters tall.

Between 1343 and 1592 the entire structure was modified inside and out by Vasari, Buontalenti and Cronaca. The refined Renaissance interior of the palazzo contrasts with the gothic exterior. A fine *courtyard* by Michelozzo (1453) features golden columns and frescoes by Vasari and, at the center, an elegant fountain surmounted by a *genietto* by Verrocchio. The upper floors include works by artists such as Vasari, Michelangelo, Verrocchio and Benedetto da Maiano. On the first floor is the awsome **Salone dei Cinquecento** (Room of the five hundred), designed by Cronaca, with frescoes by Vasari on the walls and ceiling, representing the *Return of Granduke Cosimo I to Florence, the Cities of Tuscany under Florentine Dominion*, and the *History of the Conquest of Pisa and Siena*. There is also a sculpture group by Michelangelo, called *Victory*.

The *Studiolo di Francesco I* (Study of Francis I), designed by Vasari, features paintings by the Florentine Mannerists such as Bronzino, Santi di Tito and Stradano, as well as *statues in bronze* by Giambologna and Ammannati.

The Salone dei Cinquecento leads to the *Quartiere di Leo X* (Quarters of Pope Leo X), whose rooms are rich with paintings and frescoes dedicated to prominent members of the Medici family.

On the second floor are the *Quartiere di Eleanora di Toledo* and the Quartiere degli Elementi, both by Vasari, and the *Quartiere dei Priori*. Finally, down the second staircase is the *Quartiere del Mezzanino* by Michelozzo, made up of seven rooms, of which only three are open to the public, and a study.

The Salone dei Cinquecento in Palazzo Vecchio.

The Palazzo Vecchio or Palazzo della Signoria.

THE UFFIZI GALLERY
(Galleria degli Uffizi)

The Galleria degli Uffizi is housed in a palazzo designed by Giorgio Vasari in 1560 as administrative offices ('uffizi') for the Medici family. It is among the most sumptuous and famous painting museums in the world, since it offers the visitor a complete view of Italian painting until the end of the 18th century. In addition, it is possible to admire numerous collections of the Flemish schools, famous self-portraits, antique sculptures, and a great assortment of tapestries.

In 1581 Francesco I ordered the first collection of works, to which were later added the collections brought together by several generations of the Medici family.

On the ground floor are frescoes of famous people by Andrea del Castagno, the Archaeologist, a bronze by Giorgio de Chirico, and a fresco of the *Annunciation* by Sandro Botticelli. On the first floor is the Drawings and **Prints Room**. On the second floor are sculptures and paintings arranged in 45 rooms, which open along the corridors corresponding to the three sides of the palace.

In the first rooms are works by Cimabue, Giotto, Duccio di Buoninsegna, Paolo Uccello, Simone Martini and Pietro Lorenzetti. The second room features: the *Madonna Rucellai* by Duccio di Buoninsegna (1285), which still looks "byzantine-like," despite the presence of some realistic portions; the late-13th century *Maestà di Santa Trìnita* by Cimabue, in which the search for depth and volume marks the departure from the strong influence exercised on Italian art by Byzantine models; the *Madonna di Ognissanti* by Giotto (1310), in which the figures of the angels, with their manifest spiritual materiality, testify to the enormous progress made by Giotto in the search for depth. The following two rooms are dedicated respectively to Filippo Lippi, whose *Madonna and Child* is displayed, and Antonio Pollaiolo.

The **Sala del Botticelli** features several works by Sandro Botticelli, the artist who best typifies the spirit of the first Florentine Renaissance. Among his paintings are *La Primavera*, which expresses the process of deification through love, and the *Birth of Venus*, where the Goddess appears to contain in herself a new formulation of the Absolute, in which the love of Good is coupled with the love of Beauty.

The **Sala di Leonardo** contains the *Adoration of the Magi and the Annunciation* by Leonardo da Vinci, as well as other works by artists such as Perugino, Signorelli, Verrocchio, and Lorenzo di Credi. The next rooms bring together paintings which span the period from the 16th century to the 18th century, including the *Tondo Doni* by Michelangelo, the Madonna of the Goldfinch and the portrait of *Leo X* by Raphael, the *Venus d'Urbino* by Titian, *Leda and the Swan* by Tintoretto and the *Young Bacchus* by Caravaggio. Among the foreign artists are Dürer, Rembrandt, Rubens, Van Dyck, H.Van der Goes, El Greco, Velázquez and Delacroix.

The Courtyard of the Uffizi.

The Duke of Urbino by Piero della Francesca.

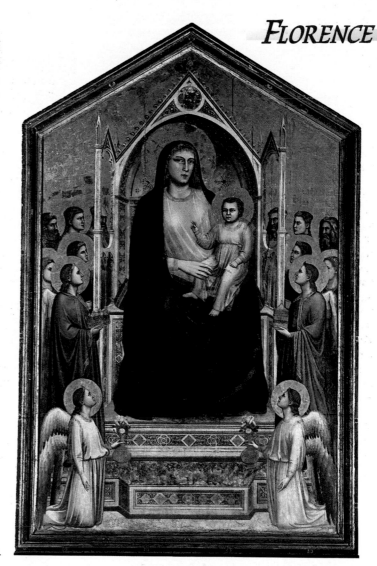

The Madonna di Ognissanti by Giotto.

The Annunciation by Leonardo da Vinci.

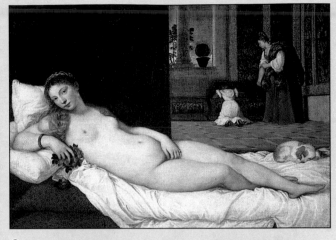

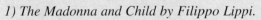

1) *The Madonna and Child by Filippo Lippi.*
2) *The Venus d'Urbino by Titian.*
3) *The Young Bacchus by Caravaggio.*
4) *Springtime by Sandro Botticelli.*

The Museo Nazionale del Bargello. Interior.

PALAZZO E MUSEO NAZIONALE DEL BARGELLO

So named because it was the residence of the podestà and the head of the police (Bargello), this palace was built in 1255, incorporating the preexisting *tower* called the *Volognana*. The *courtyard*, adorned by a portico and a loggia, conserves various sculptures, which date from the 15th to the 17th century, and come from the Boboli Gardens, Palazzo Vecchio and various Florentine churches. The museum is among the most important in Italy because of the variety of works that it contains, including paintings and sculptures by artists such as Donatello, Michelangelo, Verrocchio and Della Robbia, medieval French ivory pieces and weapons from the 14th to the 16th centuries.

On the ground floor are Florentine sculptures from the 16th century, such as the *Tondo Pitti*, the *Bacchus*, the *David-Apollo* and the *Brutus*, all works by Michelangelo.

On the first floor is the **Salone del Consiglio Generale**, also called the **Salone di Donatello** (1340-45), with ample cross-vaulting. Works here by Donatello are the lion *Marzocco*, which is the symbol of Florence, the bronze *David*, shown with a meditative expression and his foot on the head of Goliath, and finally *St. George*, in his original niche, brought from the facade of Orsanmichele.

The second floor is rich with rooms. The **Sala di Giovanni Della Robbia**, with splendid polychromatic terracottas, among them the *Adoration of the Virgin and the Presepio* (nativity scene); the **Sala di Andrea Della Robbia** contains the noteworthy *Madonna degli Architetti* (of the Architects) and the *Madonna del Cuscino* (of the Cushion); the **Sala dei bronzetti** (small bronzes), with over a thousand pieces; the **Sala delle armi** (of the weapons) and the **Sala del Verrocchio**, with sculptures from the second half of the 15th century. At the center of this room is Verrocchio's famous bronze *David*, not in the least like Donatello's David. There is also Pollaiolo's *Bust of a Young Boy* in terracotta, Verrocchio's *Bust of Lorenzo de' Medici* in terracotta, and Francesco Laurana's Bust of *Battista Sforza*.

1) The David by Donatello. 2) The Apollo by Michelangelo. 3) The Tondo Pitti by Michelangelo.
4) The Bacchus by Michelangelo. 5) The Brutus by Michelangelo.

BASILICA DI SANTA CROCE

The Basilica of Santa Croce (Holy Cross) is one of the most celebrated monuments in town, not only for its architecture and frescoes, but also for the tombs of illustrious men such as Foscolo, Dante, Alfieri, Machiavelli, Michelangelo and others. The construction of the church, begun in 1295 by Arnolfo di Cambio, was completed in the second half of the 14th century. Nonetheless, when it was consecrated by Pope Eugenius VI in as late as 1443, it was still without a facade, campanile and other elements. The *facade* by Nicolò Matas and the *campanile* by Gaetano Baccani are both neo-Gothic works from the last century. The *interior* of the marvelous basilica is striking in its scale, but can nonetheless be taken in with a single glance from any vantage point.

To the right a bit further from the entrance is the *tomb of Michelangelo*, designed by Vasari; the *cenotaph of Dante Alighieri* follows. At the third altar is a *monument to Vittorio Alfieri* by Canova, in front is the *pulpit* by Benedetto da Maiano; the *tomb of Niccolò Machiavelli*, by Spinazzi, comes next; the niche with the high relief of the *Annunciation* is a masterpiece by Donatello. In front of the sixth pilaster is the *tomb of Leonardo Bruni* (died in 1444), humanist and chancellor of the Florentine Republic and adjacent, the *tomb* of the musician *Rossini* (died in 1868); further ahead, at the sixth altar, is the *tomb of Ugo Foscolo*. The Cappella Castellani, in the right arm of the transept, is decorated with fine frescoes representing the Stories of the Saints, by Agnolo Gaddi.

At the head of the transept is the *Cappella Baroncelli*, with frescoes of the *story of the Virgin* by Taddeo Gaddi. The *Sacristy*, built on a square plan, faces the *Cappella Rinuccini*, frescoed with *Stories from the lives of the Magdalene and the Virgin* by Giovanni da Milano.

The marvelous **Cappella Maggiore**, in the center, is decorated in glass and frescoes (1380) by Agnolo Gaddi which describe episodes relating to the story of the *Invention of the true Cross* (which gives the church its name), taken from the "Legenda aurea" (Golden Legend) by Jacopo da Varagine. The painted *crucifix* is attributed – without certainty -- to the Master of Figline.

Leaving the church, the entrance to the *cloister* is just to the left; at the back of it is the Renaissance **Pazzi Chapel**, begun by Brunelleschi in 1430 for Andrea de' Pazzi, although the facade as it appears now dates to 1478. The *doorway* is by Benedetto da Maiano.

The Duomo, the Bell Tower and the Baptistery.

THE DUOMO

The Duomo, or Basilica of *Santa Maria del Fiore* (the Madonna of Florence) was designed in 1296 by Arnolfo di Cambio to replace the preexisting Church of Santa Reparata. When Arnolfo died in 1303, the work continued under Giotto, Andrea Pisano, Francesco Talenti, and finally Brunelleschi, who projected the splendid *dome*, finished in 1436.

The original *facade* by Arnolfo di Cambio, was demolished in 1587. The current Gothic style facade, built between 1871 and 1887, is the work of Emilio de Fabris. The Duomo, which had been conceived of as a meeting place as well as a church, once hosted readings of Dante's Divine Comedy. There were also other events: in 1439 the reunification with the Eastern church was decided here, and in 1441 the "Certame Coronario" took place here, a discussion held by Leon Battista Alberti in defense of literature in the vulgate. The Duomo is the fourth largest church in the world, 153 meters long by 38 meters wide. The majestic *interior*, in three naves, is rich in works of art, including stained *glass*

windows by Ghiberti, on the inside of the facade; the fresco of the *Last Judgment* by Vasari and Zuccari, on the inside of the dome; and the *sarcophagus of St. Zenobius*, first bishop of Florence, by Ghiberti, in the central chapel. Above the altar are two beautiful *kneeling angels* in enameled terracotta by Luca della Robbia. In the left nave are equestrian portraits of *Giovanni Acuto (*Sir John Hawkwood) by Paolo Uccello and *Niccolò da Tolentino* by Andrea del Castagno; the niche with *Joshua* by Ciuffagni, Donatello and Nanni di Bartolo; and the paintings with *Sts. Cosma and Damian* by Bicci di Lorenzo.

Stairs lead down to the **Crypt of Santa Reparata**, which contains the remains of the frescoes that once adorned the church, several fragments of mosaic and terracotta floor, and the *tomb of Brunelleschi*.

Behind the apse of the Cathedral is the **Museo dell'Opera** del Duomo, where various works from the Duomo, Campanile and Baptistery are on display. The best known piece in the museum is the **Pietà** by Michelangelo (1550), surely the most dramatic of the four versions of the "Pietà" sculpted by the great artist.

The facade of the Duomo.

ble. The Renaissance *bronze doors* of the Baptistery, placed at the cardinal points, are universally famous. The **Southern Door**, by Andrea Pisano (1330), evokes the Life of *St. John the Baptist* and depicts the *Allegories of the Virtues*. To make the doors more sumptuous, Pisano decided on gilded decorations. The **Northern Door** by Lorenzo Ghiberti, dates to 1403; there are scenes of the *Life of Christ* and eight reliefs with the Fathers of the Church and the Evangelists.

The **Eastern Door**, which Michelangelo called the "The Gate of Paradise" is by Ghiberti, who in ten large separate panels depicted scenes from the Old Testament. Aside from the niches with sybils and prophets, the particularity of these reliefs lies in the artist's presentation of more than one episode in each panel, thereby maintaining the unity of the story.

The *interior*, on an octagonal plan, features floors decorated with oriental motifs and magnificent 13th-century *mosaics* in inlaid glass, in the apse and cupola. To the right is the tomb of the *anti-pope John XXIII*, by Donatello (1427). In addition, there are two *Roman sarcophagi*, a *sarcophagus of Bishop Ranieri* and a *Statue of the Baptist*.

The Gate of Paradise.

CAMPANILE DI GIOTTO

The Gothic campanile (bell tower), which rises on the right of the Duomo, was begun by Giotto in 1334 and finished at the end of the 14th century by Andrea Pisano, Francesco Talenti and other artists. It stands 84 meters tall and is entirely decorated in hexagons and rhomboids, and by niches with statues of *Prophets*, *Sybils* and the *Baptist* (the originals can be found in the Museo dell'Opera del Duomo). The lower bas-reliefs represent the *Creation of Man and the Arts and Industries*; those above represent the *Planets*, the *Virtues*, the *Liberal Arts*, and the *Sacraments*.

BATTISTERO DI SAN GIOVANNI

The 11th-century *Baptistery* stands above an ancient Roman building, probably a large "domus", and remained in use until just after the Second World War. Many famous people, Dante among them, were baptized here. Several steps originally led up to the entrance, but they have disappeared with the rising street level. The external decoration, in geometric patterns, is in strips of white and green mar-

The ceiling of the Baptistery.

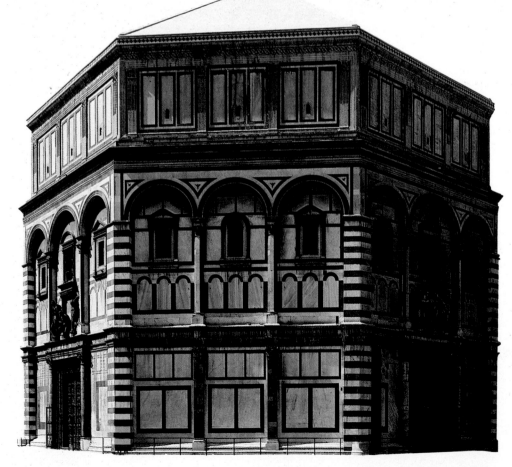

The Baptistery of St. John.

The Tomb of Lorenzo De' Medici by Michelangelo.

The Madonna Medici by Michelangelo.

BASILICA DI SAN LORENZO

The original 4th-century church was consecrated as a cathedral in 393 by Ambrogio, bishop of Milan. It was later rebuilt on the request of bishop Gherardo di Borgogna and re-consecrated in 1059, when he became Pope Nicholas II.

In 1418, the Medici commissioned a radical renovation from Filippo Brunelleschi to make it their family church; the richest families of the neighbourhood were allowed to contribute to the construction costs by building their family chapels inside. After the death of Brunelleschi in 1446, the church was finished in by Antonio Manetti in 1461. The complex was then enlarged with the *Library* and the *Mausoleum* called the "**Chapel of the Princes**", built by the patrons of the Medici family to celebrate their dynasty.

The simple *facade*, in undressed stone, does not hint at the rich interior. Upon entering, the visitor is immediately struck by the sobriety and the perfection of Brunelleschi's dimensions, based on mathematical proportions.

The space is divided in three naves by two rows of columns which sustain six round arches. Each arch corresponds, in the minor naves, to a chapel proceeded by three steps.

On the wall between the last chapel of the right nave and the transept is the marble *Altar of the Sacrament*, by Desiderio da Settignano, made up of three elements: the *Pietà*, the two *kneeling angels holding the candles* and the *Benedictory Baby*. In front, in the middle nave, are two *pulpits* by Donatello, with beautiful bronze panels.

At the end of the left transept, a 15th-century inlaid door leads to the *Old Sacristy*, one of the most complete and coherent creations of the first Florentine Renaissance. It was designed by Brunelleschi and features stucco decoration by Donatello.

To the right of the exit of the basilica is the entrance to the **Cloister** of the convent, with the stupendous **Laurentian Library** by Michelangelo. It is also possible to visit the complex of the so-called **Medici Chapels**, which can be entered around the back side of the church, and are composed of the sumptuous *Cappella dei Principi*, decorated with precious stones gathered from around the world, and the *New Sacristy*, considered to be among Michelangelo's most expressive works. Conceived as integral parts of the space, the sculptures include: the *tomb of Lorenzo il Magnifico and his brother Giuliano*, upon which rest the *Statue of the Madonna and Child*; the monument to *Giuliano, Duke of Nemours*, son of Lorenzo il Magnifico, with the statues of *Day* and *Night*; the monument to *Lorenzo, Duke of Urbino*, with the statues of *Dawn* and *Dusk*.

SANTA MARIA NOVELLA

Begun in 1246 by the architects Sisto and Ristoro, both Dominican friars, the church was finished by Jacopo Talenti in 1360 and consecrated sixty years later by Pope Martin V. The harmonious *facade*, in white and green marble, was designed by Leon Battista Alberti in the 15th century. The Romanesque-Gothic *interior*, on a Latin-cross plan, is divided into three naves by pilasters which support pointed arches and stuccoed cross vaults. In the right transept is the **Rucellai Chapel**, with a *Madonna and Child* by Nino Pisano on the altar. The adjacent **Bardi Chapel** is also known as the Chapel of St. Gregory of the Sacrament and of St. Dominic. In the niche in the wall above the altar of the **Gondi Chapel** is Brunelleschi's celebrated *Crucifix*, sculptured in polychromatic wood. At the center is the **Tornabuoni** (or **Main**) **Chapel**, dedicated to the Assumption, decorated by Ghirlandaio with frescoes representing the *Life of the Virgin* and the *Life of St. John the Baptist*.

A stairway on the left transept leads to the **Strozzi Chapel**, decorated with frescoes by Nardo di Cione and by a beautiful *polypty*ch by Andrea Orcagna on the altar.

In the left nave is Masaccio's marvelous *Trinità* (1427). In making this fresco, Masaccio applied the new rules of mathematical perspective determined by Brunelleschi. The *Crucifix* in the Sacristy is an early work by Giotto.

On the left of the facade of the church is the entrance to the Museum of Santa Maria Novella, with two cloisters: the **chiostro Grande**, frescoed by Florentine masters from of the 15th and 16th centuries, and the more beautiful **chiostro Verde**, named for the green color which dominates the frescoes by Paolo Uccello.

The interior of the Church Santa Maria Novella.

The facade of the Church Santa Maria Novella.

The Crucifixion by Beato Angelico.

theologian *Girolamo Savonarola*, who was the prior of the convent.
  On the right side of the third corridor is the magnificent **library**, by Michelozzo.

ACCADEMIA GALLERIES

The Gallery is commonly known for the numerous sculptures by Michelangelo rather than its many important Florentine paintings from the 14th through the 17th centuries.

The **Galleria dei Prigioni** contains the four sculptures of the *Prisoners*, upon which Michelangelo worked in 1530, as well as his *St. Matthew* (1503). The Prisoners are the *young slave* (first on the right); the *awakening slave* (first on the left); the *bearded slave* (second on the right); and the *Atlas* (second on the left).

These disturbing figures are unfinished works in which the bodies seem to struggle to free themselves in a dramatic and tortured scene. Michelangelo worked on them over forty years without ever finishing, leaving the observer to

THE CHURCH OF SAN MARCO

The Church and one wing of the **Convent** of San Marco, on the piazza of the same name, have a *facade* by Fra' G.B. Paladini. The rest of the complex, however, was commissioned from the Florentine architect Michelozzo by Cosimo il Vecchio in 1437. The single nave *interior* was nonetheless renovated by Giambologna and Silvani in 1579, according to Counter Reformation precepts.

Also noteworthy are the Mannerist paintings (1580) in the **Cappella di Sant'Antonino**, one of the most important architectural works by Giambologna.

The **museum** housed in the convent features the celebrated works of Beato Angelico. On the walls at the top of the stairway to the first floor are the *Annunciation* (on one side), and the *Crucifixion of St. Dominic* (on the other). From there, three corridors wind their way through the convent and around the cloister, leading to cells with other works by Beato Angelico. Among the most beautiful, in the first corridor on the left, are the *Annunciation*, the *Transfiguration* and the *Incoronation of the Virgin*; on the right, one of his most famous paintings, the *Madonna delle Ombre* (of the Shadows). At the end of the next corridor are the cells that once belonged to the Dominican

The Annunciation by Beato Angelico.

The David by Michelangelo.

**ACCADEMIA
GALLERY
*MICHELANGELO***

1) *The Young Slave.*
2) *The Pietà da Palestrina.*
3) *Atlas.*
4) *The Bearded Slave.*
5) *The Awakening Slave.*

imagine the final result. They were originally designed to be placed in the niches of the tomb which Pope Julius II had commissioned for himself. But the initial project was modified several times before becoming Julius II's actual tomb, now in the church of San Pietro in Vincoli in Rome. The statue of *St. Matthew* is also an unfinished work. It was to be one of the twelve apostles destined to adorn the buttresses in the external apses of the Duomo. In an apse at the end of the Prisoners Gallery is the famous **David**, sculpted between 1502 and 1504, and the symbol of the city. Next to the *bearded slave* is the famous *Pietà da Palestrina*.

The splendid Galleria dell'Accademia also includes the **Sale Fiorentine** (Florentine Rooms) which contain Florentine paintings from the 15th century, including the *Visitation*, one of Perugino's first works in Florence; *Tebaides*, attributed to Paolo Uccello; *Santa Barbara* by Cosimo Rosselli; the *Madonna and Child*; *St. John and two Angels* by Botticelli and the *Madonna of the Sea*, presumably by Filippino Lippi; also worthy of attention is the great **Sala della Gipsoteca Bartolini**, a collection of plas-

ter casts dedicated to the 19th-century sculpture master Bartolini, as well as the **Sale Bizantine**.

The work of Lorenzo Monaco and other Florentine painters of the 14th and 15th centuries are displayed in four rooms on the first floor.

PONTE VECCHIO

The Ponte Vecchio, which crosses the Arno at its narrowest point, is the oldest bridge in Florence. Proceeded by a Roman-era bridge and reconstructions which collapsed in 1117 and in 1333, the sturdy structure we see today was built by Neri di Fioravante, and dates to 1345. The tiny shops of gold merchants (in the middle ages there were fishmongers, butchers and leather shops) and the small houses on the sides of the bridge are its most characteristic feature.

Above, supported by arches, is the *Corridor*, built by Vasari to allow Cosimo I to walk undisturbed between the Palazzo Vecchio and the Pitti Palace.

The Ponte Vecchio on the Arno.

The facade of Palazzo Pitti.

The Gardens and Palazzo Pitti.

PALAZZO PITTI

The dimensions of the rusticated stone building (205 meters long and 36 meters high) make the Palazzo Pitti (Pitti Palace) one of the largest Florentine palaces. Today it houses eight museums and several rich collections, mainly from the 16th to the 17th centuries.

The construction was apparently begun by Filippo Brunelleschi in 1458 for the rich Florentine merchant and banker Luca Pitti, but was interrupted many times over the centuries, and finally completed in 1839.

The main entrance leads through an atrium to the *courtyard*, built by Bartolomeo Ammannati for Cosimo I in 1560. The *scalone* (grand stairway), also by Ammannati, leads to a vast first floor *vestibule* and the entrance to the **Galleria Palatina**, which contains painting and sculpture belonging to the family collection, and to the **Royal Apartments**, a series of sumptuous rooms with rich furnishings and decoration. The scalone continues up to the second floor and the **Galleria di Arte Moderna**, which includes thirty rooms rich in paintings and some sculpture, from Neoclassicism to the 20th century.

The **Museum of Costume and Porcelain** and the **Museum of the Carriages** are reached from the nearby Boboli Gardens.

GALLERIA PALATINA

The Galleria Palatina preserves part of the immense artistic legacy of the Medici (for the most part paintings) which could not be accommodated in the Galleria degli Uffizi, making it a sort of counterpart to the more famous gallery. The collection is made up of Italian and European masterpieces from the 16th and 17th centuries.

The richest portion is made up of works by Raphael, Andrea del Sarto and Titian. In addition to the more than 500 paintings on display, there are also ancient and modern sculptures and many vases arranged on tables. The Galleria also contains a great number of remarkable paintings by Dutch artists of the 17th century, which are very interesting not only because of their fine quality, but also because of the rarity of this genre in Italian collections.

In one of the first rooms, the **sala di Venere**, is the Venus Italica sculpted by Antonio Canova. The room also includes masterpieces by Titian, such as *The Concert*, the *Portrait of Julius II* and the *Portrait of Pietro Aretino*, and two admirable landscapes by Rubens, *The return from the hay fields* and *Ulysses on the Phaecian Isle*.

Two other world-famous paintings by Titian are in the **sala di Apollo**: the *Portrait of a Gentleman* and the *Magdalene*. The vault of the **sala di Marte** is decorated by a large fresco by Pietro da Cortona which features a *Medici crest*. There are also two works by Rubens, *The Consequences of War* and *The Four Philosophers*. In addition there is a *Portrait of a Man* by Veronese and the *Portrait of Cardinal Bentivoglio* by Van Dyck.

In the **sala di Giove** is the famous *Velata* by Raphael, which depicts his lover, la Fornarina (the baker's daughter).

Finally, numerous celebrated works by Raphael are displayed in the **sala di Saturno**, such as the *portraits of Agnolo and Maddalena Doni* (about 1506), the *Madonna della Seggiola* (of the chair) and the *Madonna del Granduca*; and the **sala dell'Iliade** with the portrait of a lady called the *Gravida* (pregnant woman), also by Raphael.

The Madonna del Granduca by Raphael.

The Madonna della Seggiola by Raphael.

The Veiled Woman by Raphael.

GIARDINO DI BOBOLI

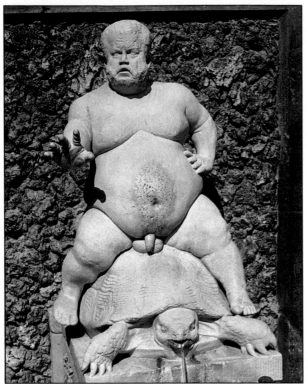

This typical Italian garden was designed in 1549 by Niccolò Tribolo; it is laid out on terraces behind the Palazzo Pitti, on the Boboli Hill, with fountains, groves, paths, and cypresses, grottoes and an amphitheater. At the end of a path to the left of Palazzo Pitti is the *Grotta grande*, created by Buontalenti (1587-97), with painted and sculpted scenes, statues, and rooms decorated with vases.

The most notable fountains in the garden are: the *Fountain of the Artichoke*, by Francesco Susini and Francesco del Tadda (1641); the *Fountain of the Small Bacchus*, by Valerio Cioli, placed near the grotto of Buontalenti (the Bacchus riding a turtle represents the dwarf Morgante, jester of the court of Cosimo I); the *Fountian of the Pitchfork*, by Stoldo Lorenzi; and Giambologna's *Fountain of the Ocean* (1576), placed among plenty of decorative plants on the island at the center of the small pond which occupies most of the *Piazzale dell'Isolotto*.

From here, a large path called the *viottolone*, lined with century-old cypresses and sculpture, leads to the top of the hill.

The Small Bacchus.   *The Boboli Gardens.*

THE CHURCH OF SAN MINIATO AL MONTE

The Romanesque church rises on the summit of the hill called the Monte alle Croci. Apparently a church dedicated to San Miniato the martyr, entrusted to a monk, was established here as early as the 8th century. It was built over the tomb of the saint, martyred in 250 under the Emperor Decius. According to legend, the decapitated Miniato found his head and placed it on the hill where the hermitage stood. The current structure was built for Bishop Hildebrand in 1018, but was probably realised in several phases and finished in 1207, the date carved into the floor. Initially belonging to Benedictine nuns, it passed to the Olivetans in 1373.

Like the Baptistery, the *facade* is covered with green and white marble. The lower part, which dates to the 11th century, is made up of five blind round arches on Corinthian half-columns, while the upper part (12th-century) has a less unified character. At the center is a window and niche with rich sculptural decoration; above, there is a mid-13th century mosaic with the *Benedictory Christ enthroned between Mary and San Miniato.*

The **campanile** was not part of the original structure, but was designed by Baccio d'Agnolo and completed in 1535. The *interior* of the church is divided into three naves. In the center, the floor is in inlaid marble with motifs of vegetables, symbolic animals and signs of the zodiac.

At the end of the nave is Michelozzo's beautiful *Chapel of the Crucifix* (1448). The paintings are by Agnolo Gaddi, while the large roses on the ceiling coffers and the polychromatic decoration along the outside of the arch are by Luca della Robbia. Across one of the two stairways is the elevated *Presbytery*, subdivided into three naves by two pairs of monolithic marble columns. To the right of the presbytery is the **Sacristy**, decorated in 1387 by Spinello Aretino. The sixteen frescoes illustrate the *Stories of St. Benedict.* In the vault are the *Four Evangelists.*

Beside the stairway in the left nave is the **Chapel of the Cardinal of Portugal** or of **San Jacopo**, built between 1459 and 1573 for Cardinale Jacopo di Lusitania, according to a design by Antonio di Manetto. In the vault are five terracotta medallions by Luca della Robbia representing the *Cardinal Virtues* and the *Holy Spirit.* On the right is the *Monument of the Cardinal* (1461), and in front an austere *throne* by Antonio Rossellino. The **crypt** is the oldest part of the church. The thirty-six small columns were gilded by Taddeo Gaddi in 1342. The *altar* contains the bones of San Miniato. On the vaults of the presbytery are figures of *saints*, *martyrs*, *virgins*, *prophets* and *evangelists* painted on a golden background by Taddeo Gaddi.

The Church of San Miniato al Monte. Interior.

The facade of Church of San Miniato al Monte.

Panorama of Florence from Piazzale Michelangelo.

PIAZZALE MICHELANGELO

Viale dei Colli leads 8 km. up to *Piazzale Michelangelo*, a square from which it is possible to enjoy an inspiring panoramic view of the city.

The panoramic view from this square is inspiring: the heart of the city in all its shapes and colors extends before your eyes, with the hill town of Fiesole in the background.

At the center of the Square, built in 1875 according to a design by the architect Giuseppe Poggi, are copies of the *David* (the original is in the Galleria dell'Accademia) and the *four allegorical statues* which decorate the MediciNew Sacristy at the church of San Lorenzo.

The *Iris Garden* at the corner of the Viale and Piazzale Michelangelo, with over 2.500 varieties of irises (the symbol of Florence), should not be missed.

PISA

Pisa is a splendid city of art, a prestigious cultural and industrial center, and home to a famous University. It sits upon a large loop of the Arno and is about 12 km. from the sea, to which the city is forever linked.

From the 11th to the 13th century, Pisa was one of the most powerful maritime republics in Italy, developing an intense merchant trade with commercial and cultural connections with many Mediterranean countries. After being defeated by Genoa at Meloria (1284), Pisa suffered a period of decline in its naval power, but thrived again under the Grand dukes of Tuscany.

The city won fame in the cultural and artistic arenas, scholarship flourished, and Galileo Galilei (1564-1642), began a tradition of scientific excellence that continues today.

In the artistic field, Pisa boasts notable buildings and works of art, but without a doubt, the most important complex is in the piazza known as the *Campo dei Miracoli*, a vast expanse of grass on the north-eastern side of the old part of the city, near the medieval walls. It is home to the *Cathedral*, the *Campanile* (commonly called the *Leaning Tower*), the *Baptistery* and the *Camposanto* (graveyard), all built between the mid-11th century and the mid-14th century.

The Duomo with the famous Leaning Tower of Pisa.

PISA

The Cathedral - The *Cathedral* or *Duomo* is the greatest example of Romanesque-Pisan architecture.
It was begun in 1064 by Buscheto and enlarged in the 12th century by Rainaldo who added the notable *facade*, which features four orders of small loggias and three bronze doorways, and is rich with sculpture and polychromatic decoration.
The majestic *interior* is divided into five naves by columns with Corinthian capitals. At the end of the central nave is the 14th-century Italian-Gothic *pulpit* by Giovanni Pisano. Among the many works inside are the bronze *chandelier* (1587), called *of Galileo*, a *Crucifix* by Giambologna, the *tomb of Arrigo VII of Luxembourg* attributed to Tino di Camaino and the urn with the remains of San Ranieri, the patron saint of the church. The *Sagrestia dei Cappellani* contains the *Treasury* of the Duomo.
At the rear of the church, the *door of San Ranieri*, by Bonanno Pisano (1186), leads to the front of the *Campanile Leaning Tower* of Pisa.

Leaning Tower of Pisa.

The *Campanile* or *Leaning Tower* of Pisa, famous for the slant that prevents it from reaching its intended height of 70 meters, stands just 54.8 meters above the ground. It was begun in 1173 by Bonanno

The Baptistery.

Pisano and finished by the end of the 14th century by Tommaso Pisano, after work was suspended when the ground subsided due to its alluvial nature. Noteworthy are the six levels of loggette with columns which stand on a marble base with blind arches in pure Pisan style, and bind up the cylindrical body of the building. From atop the tower, Galileo Galilei made many of his experiments on gravity. Recently, several excavations at the base have brought to light the remains of an ancient Etruscan sanctuary.

The Baptistery - The *Baptistery* is a circular Romanesque building, decorated by arches and loggette, culminating in a remarkable pyramidical cupola. The construction work began in 1153 under Diotisalvi, and later continued by Nicola and Giovanni Pisano.
The *interior* is 35,5 meters in diameter and contains a 13th-century *pulpit* and *statues*, also by Nicola Pisano and his son Giovanni, and a *splendid baptismal font* by Guido da Como, with the great octagonal basin completely inlaid with polychromatic marble.

The *Camposanto* - The **graveyard** was laid out in 1278 by Giovanni di Simone to hold the remains of the city's most illustrious citizens, and is marked on the outside by a ring of marble walls and blind arcades, with two doorways.
The *interior* is made up of a rectangular area surrounded by a portico with intertwining, slender Gothic arches. The walls of the portico preserve several frescoes, among the few which survived the bombing of July, 1944. They represent *Biblical scenes* by Benozzo Gozzoli, *Stories from the life of San Ranieri* by Andrea Bonaiuti and other frescoes by Taddeo Gaddi and Spinello Aretino.
In addition, there are sculptures by Giovanni Pisano and Tino di Camaino, Roman *sarcophagi of the Sponsali* and *of Phaedra and Hippolytus*, and the *Inconsolable*, a 19th-century sculpture by Bartolini.

The Leaning Tower.

SIENA

Founded by the Etruscans and later a Roman province, Siena became an important center when the roads descending from the other side of the Alps joined to become the *Via Francigena* (or *Romea*, from the name of the pilgrims who went to Rome), which passed through the town and served as the principle artery between Northern Italy and Rome.

The city reached its maximum splendour between the 11th and 13th centuries, when it managed to exercise its economic power in Europe and to prevail in frequent wars with Florence.

The Sienese silver currency contributed to the city's commercial development, which was based essentially on wax, textiles, dying, spices, and metal used for coins which was supplied by the mines of Montieri.

In these years of great political and economic stability, several important architectural works which wonderfully represent medieval Europe were built, and today render Siena one of the most beautiful cities in the world.

Palazzo Pubblico - In the period between 1287 to 1355, after the victory over the Florentines at Montaperti (1260),

the Council of Nine gained stability and authority and the city began many urban projects. Among them was the *Palazzo Pubblico*, which became the symbol of Siena. Begun at the end of the 13th century, it was subsequently finished with the soaring *Torre del Mangia*, 102 meters tall, which was built to the same height as the Duomo's bell tower to underscore the equality between civic and religious power. The interior of this palace holds the rooms of the Museo Civico, rich with numerous treasures and frescoes, among them the *Maestà* by Simone Martini (1315), in the *Sala del Mappamondo*.

After climbing the 400 steps of the tower, one is rewarded with a stunning panoramic view of the city. Interestingly, the red-coloured, shell-like **Piazza del Campo** seems to descend from the fountain *Fonte Gaia* toward the Palazzo Pubblico as if to enwrap it in a protective embrace. It is in this piazza that all the citizens celebrate the most important events, such as the great race of the Palio.

The Palio - The Palio, which takes place July 2nd and August 16th, consists of just three laps around the piazza del Campo at incredible velocity. The race is very danger-

The Baptistery.

Piazza del Campo. In the background the Palazzo Pubblico.

ous, and ends in a little less than a minute. Although brief in duration, the event and its accompanying preparations and celebrations magically bring to life the atmosphere of the medieval city and the spirit of ancient rivalries among the contrade (neighborhoods) which take part.

Of Siena's seventeen contrade, only 10 participate in the palio. A great dinner with tables in the open air lining the main streets of the victorious contrada closes the event with lengthy celebrations.

The Duomo - At Siena's high point, the city took on more ambitious urban projects than at any other time, among them the construction of what was meant to be the most grandiose cathedral in the Christian world.

At the end of the 13th century, Giovanni Pisano was chosen to renovate and enlarge the existing Duomo (1284-1299), which dated to the 12th century.

Unfortunately, Pisano was able to complete only a part of the project, which had included a facade with spires and three doors, in the style of French Gothic churches. Because of the plague of 1348, the Sienese gave up their great projects and intentions, and resigned themselves to simply finish that which had already been built. The *interior* of the cathedral is divided into three naves lined with inlaid marble floors with graffiti and panels by various artists. The white and black stripping of the columns delimiting the naves catches the eye, as does the *pulpit*, a masterpiece of Gothic sculpture by Arnolfo di Cambio and Nicola Pisano (1265 - 1269).

On the left nave is the entrance to the **Libreria Piccolomini**, with frescoes by Pinturicchio of scenes from the life of Pope Pius II and a 3rd-century Roman sculpture. The **Museo dell'Opera Metropolitana** *(Cathedral Museum)*, on the left side of the piazza, is worth visiting.

The Baptistery - The Baptistery is on Piazza San Giovanni, behind the apse of the Duomo, and serves as its crypt. It was built between 1316 and 1325 and has a Gothic facade, unfinished at the top.

The *interior*, also Gothic, is by Camaino and Tino di Crescentino and holds a beautiful 15th-century baptismal font by Jacopo della Quercia, decorated with two statues by Donatello and several bronze panels by celebrated sculptors.

The Duomo.

NAPLES

Naples and its gulf fill a natural landscape of unspeakable beauty, and can be considered the Southern metropolis par excellence. The city is among the principle seaports of the Mediterranean, and is the busiest terminal for passenger ships in Italy. But above all Naples is an art city of undisputed charm for its artistic and cultural legacies. It is therefore a great tourist attraction, at times full of strident contrasts, but still very stirring for the warm sincerity of its outgoing inhabitants, who express themselves in a colourful and musical dialect.

The ancient Neapolis, "new city", was founded by Greek colonists from Cumae in the 6th century BC, and very soon became a flourishing center, thanks to its fortunate geographical position. The city suffered the assault of rough and primitive Italic peoples (first the Lucans and the Samnites), without ever losing its own Greek civilisation. Naples was romanized in about the 4th century BC and was favoured by emperors such as Augustus, Tiberius and Nero, who built their villas and spent their long holidays in the city and its marvelous surroundings and islands, like Capri and Ischia.

After the fall of the Roman empire, Naples found itself at the center of the cruel struggle between the Byzantines and the Goths, who had invaded Italy. Finally conquered in 546 by the Byzantines, it remained in their hands until 570, the year in which it was taken by the Longobards. About two centuries later, in 763, the city created its own duchy, and began a period of great splendour, until in 1140 it was conquered by the Normans under the command of Roger II of Altaville, who made it the capital of his new kingdom.

From then until 1860, the year in which it joined the united Italy, Naples was the uninterrupted capital of an independent kingdom which knew changing fortunes and saw eight dynasties succeed to its throne. The Normans, in fact, were followed by the Swabians, who obtained the Neapolitan throne by hereditary succession with Frederick II (1194). Less than a century later, in 1266, with the decline of the power of Swabia, Naples passed to the Angevins, in whose hands the city remained for nearly two hundred years. After a long conflict, Alfonso of Aragon, known as "the Magnanimous", took the throne in 1442.

The Aragon period, during which Naples knew the splendors of the Renaissance, lasted until 1504. With the Armistice of Lyons, Naples was ceded to Spain, and remained a Spanish viceroyalty until 1713, when with the Peace of Utrecht it fell under Austrian control. The long period of foreign domination, under which the autonomous character and decorum of the city was always respected (at least formally), came to an end when the Neapolitan throne passed to the Bourbon Charles III in 1734. One of the most enlightened sovereigns, not only in Italy, but also in all of Europe, he reigned until 1759, leaving his indelible mark on the city. His successors, unfortunately, were not politically nor culturally his equal, and in 1799, under the impulse of the ideas of revolutionary France, the best of the intellectual bourgeoisie and the Neapolitan nobility created the glorious but short-lived Parthenopean Republic. Between 1806 and 1815, Giuseppe Bonaparte and later Gioacchino Murat ruled Naples, promoting great reforms.

The cruel Bourbon repression that followed in 1815 widened the gap between the dynasty and the people, so much so that when Garibaldi's Mille (thousand men) departed in 1860 to conquer the kingdom, their advance was met with the great public support, and Naples ultimately became part of the State of Italy.

Among the Neapolitan religious festivals, each characterised by rich decorations, the best known are those of the Madonna di Piedigrotta, Santa Maria del Carmine and above all the Miracle of San Gennaro. Public life centers around Piazza del Plebiscito and in the Galleria Umberto I, while the popular quarters, with their alleys decked with laundry hanging out to dry, are found in Spaccanapoli and to the west of Via Toledo.

With 1.1 million residents, Naples is the third largest city in Italy. The substantial efforts made by state and local authorities to render the city more organised, modern and increasingly serene are beginning to achieve tangible results, which vivacious Neapolitans seem to enthusiastically appreciate and optimistically welcome.

Situated on the southern part of the Sorrentine Peninsula, the Amalfi Coast can without doubt be considered one of the most beautiful coastlines in Italy. The tract, which winds a tortuous seaside road, goes from Positano to Vietri sul Mare. All along it offers the visitor an ever-changing landscape of stupendous inlets, promontories and small bays.

At the heart of this unforgettable coastline lays the town of Amalfi, which enjoys a perennially perfect climate scented with the aroma of citrus groves. The town, besides offering a marvelous view of the sea and other natural beauty, is famous for its many artisanal products.

In front of the Sorrentine Peninsula rise three islands, 17 miles from Naples, called the "isole degli dei" (islands of the gods): Capri, internationally famous for its worldliness and its waters; Ischia, island of health and nature; and Procida, wild and untouched.

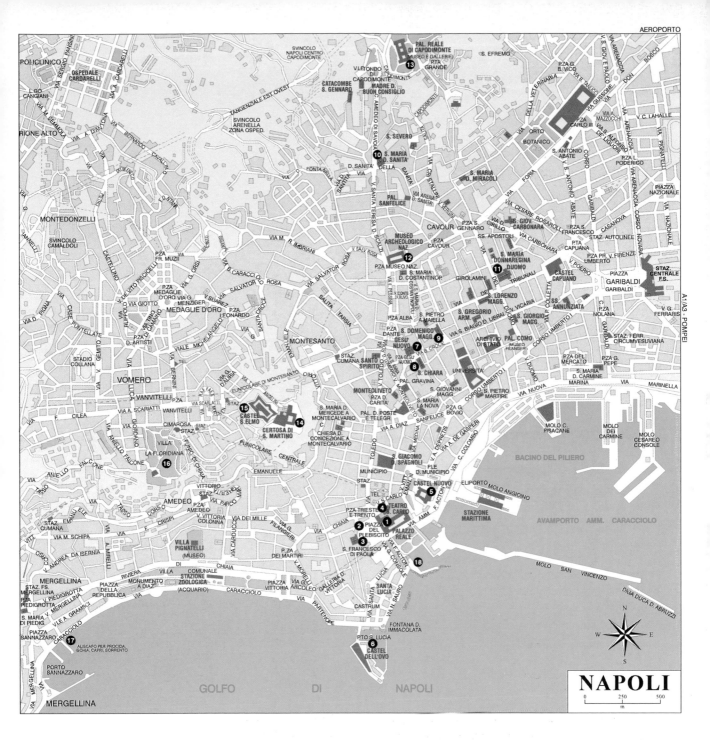

LIST OF THE MONUMENTS

1) The Royal Palace.
2) Piazza del Plebiscito.
3) San Francesco di Paola.
4) San Carlo Theatre.
5) Maschio Angioino.
6) Castel dell'Ovo.
7) The Church of the Gesù Nuovo.

8) The Church of Santa Chiara.
9) San Domenico Maggiore.
10) Santa Maria della Sanità.
11) The Duomo.
12) Museo Archeologico Nazionale.
13) Museo Reale di Capodimonte.
14) Certosa di San Martino.

15) Castel Sant'Elmo.
16) Villa Floridiana.
17) Ferries departing for Capri, Ischia and Sorrento.
18) Hydrofoils departing for Capri, Ischia and Sorrento.

PALAZZO REALE

The Palazzo Reale (Royal Palace), an imposing 17th-century structure by the celebrated architect Domenico Fontana, was rebuilt after a fire in the 19th century, and restored after having suffered great damage during World War II. The *facade* features a long portico, which originally was completely open. In the 18th century, however, because of several cracks in the walls, it was decided that alternating arches be closed and filled in with niches to increase the structural strength of the ground floor. In the 19th century, eight statues were placed in the niches, representing the kings from the different dynasties which have ruled Naples; naturally, the most significant were selected, from Roger the Norman to Victor Emanuel II of Savoy.

The *interior* of the Palazzo Reale is sumptuous: from a vast square *courtyard* by Fontana, the solemn 17th-century *Scalone d'onore (stairway of honour)* by Francesco A. Picchiatti leads to the first floor and the entrances to the *Teatro di Corte*, the *Royal Apartment* and the *Royal Chapel*.

The **Teatro di Corte**, renovated in 1768 by Ferdinando Fuga, was recently restored after grave damage suffered during World War II.

The **Royal Apartment** preserves all its sumptuousness, and is made up of a suite of 17 rooms, in which it is possible to admire Neapolitan furniture, including pieces in Baroque and Imperial style, *frescoes*, *tapestries*, *precious vases* and an important *collection of paintings*. The most notable rooms are: *Room IV*, which belonged to *Queen Maria Cristina*, with Titian's *Portrait of Pierluigi Farnese*; *Room VI* or the *Throne Room*; *Room VII*, with a *View of Venice* by Canaletto; *Room XI*, with the *Prodigal Son* by Mattia Preti; and *Room XV*, with *Jesus under the Cross* by Giorgio Vasari.

The **Royal Chapel**, built just after the mid-17th century by the architect Cosimo Fanzago and remade in the first half of the 19th century, also suffered great damage during World War II and needed a long and careful restoration. Worth noting, on the ceiling, is the airy painting by Domenico Morelli representing the *Assumption*, and the rich *main altar*, in gilded bronze and semi-precious stones.

The Palazzo Reale and Piazza del Plebiscito.

The door of the Church of St. Francis which opens onto Piazza del Plebiscito.

PIAZZA DEL PLEBISCITO

The solemn and monumental appearance of Piazza del Plebiscito arouses a certain awe in those who look upon it for the first time. Such an impression is determined, aside from the vastness of the piazza itself, by the two grandiose buildings that face each other from across the square: the *Palazzo Reale* on one side, and the *Neoclassical Church of San Francesco di Paola* on the other, in addition to the great *Palazzo della Prefettura* to the north, and that of the *Principe di Salerno* to the south. Complementing the magnificence of the scene, at the center of the elliptical part of the piazza and in front of the semicircular portico of the church, stand the *equestrian statues* representing the Bourbon kings *Ferdinand I* and *Charles III*, by Antonio Cali and Antonio Canova, respectively.

The piazza, by now a symbol of Naples, is often the site of concerts and public celebrations. On Sundays and holidays you are likely to see numerous young newlywed couples posing for a traditional photo on the piazza.

SAN FRANCESCO DI PAOLA

The church, built for Ferdinando I to celebrate his return to the kingdom of Naples after the Napoleonic interlude of Gioacchino Murat, clearly recalls two celebrated Roman monuments: the Pantheon for the actual church, and the Colonnade in St. Peter's Square for the elliptical portico in Doric style, which departs from both sides of the church. The plan of San Francesco is, therefore, rather classical: the *facade* features a pronaos with six columns, each reinforced on the sides by two ionic pilasters and all surmounted by a triangular tympanum, as in the ancient Greek and Roman temples. Across the rectangular atrium is the entrance to the vast *Rotonda*, with a diameter of nearly 34 meters.

The numerous statues in the *interior* match the solemn, cold elegance so typical of neoclassical buildings. The rich *altar* in semi-precious stones and lapis lazuli is by Anselmo Cangiano, and was brought from the church of SS. Apostoli.

SAN CARLO THEATRE

The Teatro San Carlo is one of the gems of Naples, both for its aesthetic and monumental beauty and for the scores of musical history with which it is connected. Built in 1727 according to a plan by Giovanni Antonio Medrano, who also designed the Palazzo Reale di Capodimonte, it soon became the center of Neapolitan musical life, which knew its most glorious period with the flowering of the *opera buffa (comic opera)* at the end of the 18th century. The theatre was renovated and embellished many times by the major architects working in Naples between the 18th and 19th centuries, from Ferdinando Fuga to Antonio Niccolini. The *interior* is at once sumptuous and severe, with the scenographic royal section, the balustrades with 184 elegantly adorned boxes, and the grandiose fresco on the vault.

In front of the Teatro is the 19th-century **Galleria Umberto I**. Vast and elegant, it is surmounted by a dome of iron and glass, over 56 meters tall.

The Galleria Umberto I.

The interior of the San Carlo Theatre .

MASCHIO ANGIOINO OR CASTEL NUOVO

The Maschio Angioino is a ponderous building erected for the Angevin Charles I at the end of the 13th century in a dominating position, and later rebuilt under Alfonso I of Aragon. Here resided the sumptuous and refined courts of both the Angevin and Aragonese dynasties, which successively ruled the city. The western side of the castle is topped with massive 15th-century cylindrical towers. Between the Torre di Mezzo and the Torre della Guardia is the splendid **Triumphal Arch**, built in the mid-15th century to celebrate the triumph of Alfonso I of Aragon, on a project which some authoritative art critics attribute to Luciano Laurana, partly because of its similarity to the celebrated facade of the Palazzo Ducale in Urbino.

In any case, the elegance of the proportions of the two superimposed arches, framed by Corinthian columns, each paired and surmounted by a sculpted attic, is undeniable. On the first arcade is *Alfonso I of Aragon* with his court, while the *Four Virtues* arc represented on the second. Up above is the finishing touch: two allegorical representations of rivers, and surmounting everything, a *statue of the Archangel St. Michael*.

The *interior* of the castle, which still constitutes a living testimony to centuries of Neapolitan history, should not be missed. The entrance is through the Triumphal Arch and across a vestibule, which houses the *bronze door* which was originally part of the arch, decorated with animated reliefs representing battle scenes. The Triumphal Arch leads through to the large four-sided *courtyard*, upon which face (from left to right) the *Room of the Barons*, *Palatine Chapel* and the *Viceroyal apartment*.

CASTEL DELL'OVO

Right in the center of the deep inlet of the Gulf of Naples, an oblong small island extends toward the sea upon which rises the ponderous site of the *Castel dell'Ovo*, one of the most typical buildings on the Neapolitan landscape. However, aside from its architectural qualities, the castle is extraordinarily important for having been a constant presence in the life of the city from its earliest times.

In fact, it sinks its roots the beginning of Parthenopean history, and has accompanied Naples through its trials and triumphs.

Castel dell'Ovo stands today on the site of the Roman era villa of the celebrated Lucullus; the pagan building was later transformed into a Christian coenobium (monastery), and in the 12th century it became a fortress used first by the Normans and then by the Swabians. The name of the castle dates more or less to this period, which is likely due to its oval design. A medieval legend, however, attributes the name to an enchanted egg, placed in the building by the Latin poet Virgil, who in the middle ages enjoyed fame as a magician. The later sovereigns of Naples, from the Angevins to the Aragonese to the Bourbons, also used the castle as a fortress or prison, according to necessity, and even today the imposing structure plays a military role.

The picturesque fishermen's houses, which together with several celebrated, typical trattorie, cling to the walls of the castle, form the **Borgo Marinaro**, a characteristic Neapolitan corner whose animated life offers a pleasant contrast with the harsh castle. The tiny island is connected to the land by a dock which embraces the **Porticciolo di Santa Lucia**, the little harbor made famous all over the world by classical Neapolitan songs.

Panorama of Naples and its Gulf, with Mt. Vesuvius in the background.

The statue of the Virgin and the Church of Gesù Nuovo.

Facade of the Church of Gesù Nuovo.

CHIESA DEL GESÙ NUOVO

The Church of the Gesù Nuovo, so-called to distinguish it from the Gesù Vecchio, is found in the Palazzo dell'Università on Piazza del Gesù Nuovo, near the *spire of the Immacolata* with *statue of the Virgin* in gilded copper on top. The *facade*, decorated by characteristic rusticated stone protruding in diamond points, is rather unique for a church: it was, in fact, the original facade of Palazzo Sanseverino, built at the end of the 15th century, and transformed into a church in the following century by the Jesuit Giuseppe Valeriani. The *interior* in three naves is in a Greek cross, and bears the mark of various celebrated architects working in Naples between the 17th and 18th centuries, such as Cosimo Fanzago, who restored and embellished the church after a fire in 1639; Arcangelo Guglielmelli and, later, Ignazio Di Nardo, who renovated the dome twice (the second time in the form of a low "bowl"); Ferdinando Fuga, who reinforced what was a weak structure with the counter-pilasters and undersides of the arches.

Among the noteworthy pictorial decorations are: a large fresco by Francesco Solimena, on the internal part of the facade, above the portal, representing *Heliodorus driven from the temple*; the frescoes on the vault of the middle nave, by Belisario Corenzio and Paolo De Matteis, who also did those on the vault of the transept; the *Visitation* on the altar of the first chapel of the right nave, by Massimo Stanzione and his assistants; the frescoes of the presbytery, representing scenes from the *Life of Mary*, also by Stanzione; and the altar in the left arm of the transept by Cosimo Fanzago. In a vast room with a separate entrance to the left of the church, is a large canvas by Guercino, representing the *Trinity and Saints*.

Detail of the facade.

THE CHURCH OF SANTA CHIARA

The church, built in the 14th century in Gothic-Provençal style, was entirely rearranged in the 18th century. The medieval structure was completely covered with extremely rich ornamentation, and decorated with grandiose frescoes by Sebastiano Conca, Francesco De Mura, Giuseppe Bonito and Paolo de Maio. All of this was destroyed during World War II.

Reconstruction after the war returned the church to its original medieval appearance, in harmony with the severe *facade*, decorated by a *pronaos* in three pointed arches and by a *doorway* in red and yellow finely inlaid marble. To the side of the facade is the *campanile*; the lower portion dates to the 14th century, while the upper part was rebuilt after it collapsed in 1456.

The **monastery** was built, together with the church, by Queen Sancia of Majorca, wife of Robert of Anjou. The visit to the monastery is particularly interesting above all for the original *cloister with majolica tiles*, decorated with vivid landscapes, festoons, and various scenes and allegories, thus forming a perfect scene with the garden at its center. It is a typical 18th century Neapolitan work, built in the middle of the century by Giuseppe and Donato Massa.

The Church of Santa Chiara.

The cloister of the Church of Santa Chiara.

Interior of San Domenico Maggiore.

The main altar in the Church of Santa Maria della Sanità.

SAN DOMENICO MAGGIORE

The church was built between 1283 and 1324 as part of the convent complex, which was a center for theological studies. The *facade* of San Domenico is decorated by a portico with a beautiful pointed marble doorway, the only remaining part of the original facade.

The *interior*, in the form of a Latin cross, preserves its original Gothic architecture only in the double line of pointed arches which divide it into three naves. Several arbitrary renovations, especially in the 19th century, left the sober skeleton of the church laden with stucco works and gilding of questionable taste. In any case, San Domenico, is nonetheless rich in precious paintings as well as history.

Along the right nave, the first chapel contains, in addition to several 14th-century tombs, a *Madonna and Child and Dominican Saints* by Francesco Solimena; in the sixth chapel, is the original *Papal Bull* from 1567, with which Pope Pius V proclaimed St. Thomas Aquinas, who had taught theology in the attached convent, Doctor of the Church. This chapel serves as a passageway to the *Cappellone of the Holy Crucifix*, also connected to the memory of St. Thomas. The 13th-century *Crucifix*, painted on wood, is known for the miracle in which Jesus spoke to St. Thomas. In the seventh chapel is a work by Giordano, the *Madonna and Child and St. Thomas*. At the end of the nave is the right arm of the transept: from the second arch, one can enter the small ancient church, which was incorporated in the new construction of San Domenico over the course of the 16th century.

In the first chapel on the left arm of the transept is the *Flagellation* by Caravaggio (1607). In the third chapel is the *sepulcher of Phillip of Anjou*, by Tino da Camaino.

SANTA MARIA DELLA SANITÀ

The church was built between 1602 and 1613 by the Dominican Friars based on a design by Giuseppe Donzelli (known as Frà Nuvolo). The *dome* is covered in majolica tiles and flanked, on the right, by a high campanile. Its vast *interior*, in the shape of a Greek cross, is stunning. Across two large marble stairways is a main altar surmounted by a beautiful *ciborium* (*canopy*). Under the altar and the apse extends the great *Cemetery Chapel of San Gaudioso*.

Here is the entrance to the paleo-christian *Catacombs* with 17th and 18th-century frescoes along the lengthy corridors. At the end of the first corridor is the tomb of San Gaudioso, who died around 450. The skulls which stick out of the walls have nothing to do with the catacombs, but instead reveal a macabre custom that dates to the 17th-century, by which cadavers were left to dry out, and were then interred in the walls with only the skull exposed.

bust which contains the skull of the Saint and two *ampullae*. These contain the *dried blood of the martyr*, which according to tradition, turns to liquid twice a year (in May and September), in an atmosphere of particular religious intensity, with great participation by the faithful.

From the left nave, a doorway decorated with sculpture leads to the ancient *Church of Santa Restituta*, incorporated into the Duomo. The structure is the oldest basilica in Naples, and dates to the 4th century.

MUSEO ARCHEOLOGICO NAZIONALE

Begun in 1585 to serve as the cavalry barracks for the the Spanish Viceroy Duke d'Ossuna, the building was later renovated and enlarged by Domenico Fontana in order to become the Palazzo degli Studi, the seat of the University. It remained that way until 1777, when Pompeo Schiantarelli, who along with Ferdinando Fuga was the most prominent architect of the period, was asked by Ferdinando IV to turn it into a museum. In addition to several collections of antiquities inherited from Elizabeth Farnese, mother of the Bourbon king Charles, the museum received the extremely rich findings which had started

Painting of the "miracle of the blood" in the Duomo.

IL DUOMO

Dedicated to San Gennaro, patron saint of Naples, and built in the 13th century in Gothic style, the *Duomo* was renovated many times, so much so that very little of it belongs to the earliest version. The *facade*, rebuilt at the end of the 19th century in pseudo-Gothic style, retains the three original *doorways* by Antonio Baboccio, which date to the first construction. The central doorway, with the beautiful *Madonna and Child* by Tino da Camaino, is especially fine.

The *interior*, in the form of a Latin cross and divided into three naves by two rows of cross-shaped pilasters, features a remarkable *middle nave*, with *frescoes* by Luca Giordano and his assistants, and a precious inlaid and gilded *wood ceiling* (1621). The *baptismal font* is an interesting piece made up by antique parts (the bowl is in Egyptian basalt) and fine 17th-century coloured marbles and bronze.

In the right nave is the **Chapel of San Gennaro**, also called the Treasury, at the entrance of which is a beautiful gate in gilded bronze by Cosimo Fanzago; the interior of the chapel, on a Greek cross plan, is surmounted by a dome with a fresco by Giovanni Lanfranco, representing *Paradise*. The other frescoes in the chapel are by Domenichino and depict *Stories from the life of San Gennaro*.

The main altar is decorated by a silver relief by Vinaccia illustrating the *Translation of the reliquary of San Gennaro from Mount Virgin to Naples*. Behind it is a *silver*

Alexander and Darius at the Battle of Issus. Mosaic from Pompeii.

Portrait of a Young Woman. Fresco from Pompeii.

The Strolling Musicians. Mosaic from Pompeii.

Paquius Proculus and his Wife. Fresco from Pompeii.

Primavera. Fresco from Pompeii.

coming from excavations made in 18th century at Herculaneum and Pompeii, not to mention the sites of Cumae, Paestum, Pozzuoli, and numerous other locations, for the most part in Campania.

The following is a brief list of the immense collection: marble and bronze statues; Egyptian and prehistoric collections; paintings and mosaics from Pompeii, Herculaneum and Stabia and an interesting model of Pompeii; precious ivory, silver and gold; vases from various necropoli; and a section on ancient technology and machines, the only one in the world made with authentic objects rather than reproductions.

The following items are especially worth noting for their exceptional artistic and documentary value: The group of the *Tirannicidi*, representing the two brothers Harmodius and Aristogeiton, a precious Roman copy of a Greek original from the 5th century BC; the imposing *Farnese Athena*, a well-made Imperial-era copy; the *Relief with Orpheus, Eurydice and Hermes* is one of the museum's masterpieces; the colossal head of the so-called *Farnese*

Juno; the celebrated *Doryphorus*, or spear bearer, from a bronze original by Polyclitus; a *Nike* or *Victory* without head or arm, yet still full of life; the *Nereids*, of particular decorative value; the beautiful *statue of the Wrestler*, signed by Koblanos of Aphrodisia; the colossal group of the *Farnese Bull*, about 4 meters tall; the refined *Venus of Capua*, a discreet Roman copy; the so-called *Psyche of Capua*, with its lovely mutilated torso, all suffused by a spiritual beauty; the warmer and more mature *Venus of Sinuessa*; the enormous *Farnese Hercules*, which belongs to the same collection that gave its name to the room; and finally, the peculiar statue which represents *Artemis (or Diana) of Ephesus*.

The **Gallery of Greek and Roman Portraits**, with the famous *Bust of Homer* and the colossal head of the Roman Emperor *Antonius Pius*, faces onto another side of the courtyard.

The famous *mosaics* from Pompeii are arranged on the first floor, and testify to the great artistic value of this particular type of figurative technique. *Consulting the*

*The Annunciation by
Filippo Lippi.
Capodimonte Museum.*

*Madonna and Child by
Sandro Botticelli.
Capodimonte Museum.*

Sorceress
by Dioscorides of Samos is finely executed and admirably characterised. The *Strolling musicians*, by the same artist, even surpasses the preceding work for its great expressiveness and beautiful colors. The two mosaics were found not far from one another in Pompeii.

Also worthy of attention is the extremely fine *Portrait of a Young Woman*, whose features, typical of the inhabitants of Campania, suggest a pensive expression. Finally, there's the very well-known *Alexander and Darius at the Battle of Issus*.

The second floor holds numerous paintings from excavations in Pompeii, Herculaneum and Stabia, some of which are particularly noteworthy from an artistic point of view, such as: the tragic figure of *Medea*, by Timomachus of Byzatium, a powerful reproduction of one of the most famous ancient paintings; the *Primavera (springtime)*, with its foreshortening of a delicate young girl collecting flowers; and the celebrated portrait of *Paquius Proculus and his Wife*, considered by experts to be the most important portrait from Pompeii, above all for the vivacious characterization of the couple, which makes them look like two typical inhabitants of modern Campania.

On the second floor there are nicely arranged collections of precious terracottas, painted vases, coins, cameos and medals, featuring pieces of inestimable value. The most precious is perhaps the *Tazza Farnese*, a finely crafted cup in sardonyx, one of the largest cameos in the world.

PALAZZO REALE DI CAPODIMONTE

Pine trees, cypresses, eucalyptus and magnolias dot the lawns of the large park which surrounds the grandiose *Royal Palace*. Begun in 1738 by the architect Giovanni Antonio Medrano and finished over a century later, the building features an imposing, long facade.

The Bourbon King Charles III wanted it to hold the art collections that had belonged to his mother, Elisabetta Farnese: between 1759 and 1806, in fact, the precious pieces of the Farnese collection, now held in the Museo Archeologico Nazionale, were on exhibit in the Royal Palace; later, its rooms housed the arms from the royal Armory, porcelain and other minor collections. After World War II, it was decided to move the paintings the Pinacoteca Nazionale here, which until then had been kept in the Archeological Museum.

On the first floor of the Palace are the **Galleria dell'Ottocento** (19th-century), the **Historic Apartment**, with the **Museum of Porcelain**, **tapestries**, **drawings and prints**, and the splendid *De Ciccio collection*.

The rooms on the first floor hold an impressive collection of porcelain and majolica from the most celebrated European manufacturers, which were once part of the furnishings of the various royal palaces in Naples.

The most important among the Museo di Capodimonte's three sections is undoubtedly the **Pinacoteca Nazionale**, arranged on the second floor. Among the most important works: *St. Ludovic of Toulouse with his brother Robert of Anjou* (1317), by the Sienese artist Simone Martini; the *Crucifixion*, by Masaccio; a *Madonna with Child and Angels* by Sandro Botticelli, worth noting for the elegance of its line and the preciousness of its color; the *Annunciation with St.John the Baptist and St.Andrew* by Filippino Lippi; the *Holy Family with a Young St. John*, and two portraits of *Pope Clemente VII* by Fra Sebastiano del Piombo.

Among the Venetian painting of the 15th and 16th centuries, worth noting above all is the powerful *Portrait of Francesco Gonzaga* by Andrea Mantegna, one of the greatest painters of the 15th century (he also painted *St. Eufemia*), and the *Transfiguration* by Giambellino (Giovanni Bellini), another 15th century masterpiece.

Titian's celebrated *Portrait of the Farnese Pope Paul III with his nephews Ottavius and Alexander* (1546) was painted as a commission for the Farnese family. In addition, there are several works by European painters, including the *Misanthrope* and the *Parable of the Blind*, both painted in 1568 by Pieter Brueghel; the *Crucifixion*, by Anton van Dyck, and the *Portrait of Charles IV, King of Spain and his wife, Maria Luisa of Parma*, Queen of Spain, painted at the end of the 18th century by one of the greatest European painters, Francisco Goya.

CAPRI

The Sorrentine Peninsula is intimately connected to the island of Capri, for the two share an identical morphology and the same geological history. Capri has appropriately been called the "gem of the Gulf of Naples," because those who settled and conquered it, over the course of the centuries, never altered the natural beauty of the island. More than in any other celebrated tourist destination, in Capri one is still struck by a notable harmony between the works of nature and of man.

Life in **Capri**, the main town which gives the island its name, concentrates on *Piazza Umberto I*, a tiny open space not much larger than a courtyard. Here some ruins of the oldest settlement in the island are still visible, such as the remnants of the calcareous walls built in the 6th and 5th centuries BC. But the charm of the little square does not belong entirely to its ruins, or its *Torre dell'Orologio (Clock Tower)*. The Piazza has the feeling of a living room in the open air, where the two sides of Capri, the fleeting international jet set and the picturesque, sincere, local ambiance come close to one another without ever touching.

The **Certosa di San Giacomo** was built between 1371 and 1375; it was rebuilt about two centuries later, after a disastrous raid by the Saracens, and subsequently restored many times. At the top of Via Tragara is the Belvedere Canon,

Marina Grande, seen from Villa San Michele.

which offers a wonderful view of the Marina Piccola inlet and of the **Tre Faraglioni**, three characteristic needle-shaped rocks emerging off the coast. It is possible to take many enjoyable walks on Capri. Particularly interesting is the excursion to the ruins of *Villa Jovis* on top of Mt. Tiberius, named after the Roman emperor that used the villa as his residence on Capri.

On the opposite side of the island, perched on a high plateau, rises **Anacapri**, the second locality of the island. The plateau served as a lookout post against Saracen invasion. until 1877, it was connected to the **Marina Grande** below only via the *Scala fenicia (Phoenician steps)*, a steep and narrow stairway made up of over 500 steps.

The discreet, quiet, charming atmosphere of Anacapri makes this little town a favourite resort among those who love serenity and peace. Among its highlights is *Villa San Michele*, built on the site of a Roman house. Aside from boasting a splendid view and a beautiful garden, the villa still houses many antique pieces.

An excursion to the most famous of the numerous caves of the island, the **Grotta Azzurra** (Blue Grotto) should not be missed. The light filters in and reflects through the water into the cave, creating a wonderful sky-blue color all around.

The Certosa di San Giacomo with the Faraglioni (rocks) in the background.

The Blue Grotto.

POMPEII

The founding of Pompeii was favoured by its fortunate location, midway between the coast and the estuary of the Sarno river, which in ancient times made an excellent landing place for sailors. The city began as an Oscan village in the 8th century BC. Shortly afterwards, Pompeii was influenced by the Greek colonies in the area and traded with the Etruscans; in 425 BC, Pompeii fell under the dominion of the warlike Samnites, who left their indelible mark on the structure and architecture of the city. After the Romans defeated the Samnites, Pompeii took on Roman customs, as well as new architectural and ornamental techniques.

On August 24th, 79 AD, Mount Vesuvius suddenly erupted. A tempest of ash, lapillus, poisonous gas, and magma fell on the areas surrounding the volcano, while streams of lava and incandescent mud continuously ran down its slopes. The catastrophe was so sudden and unexpected, that the over thirty-thousand people living in the city below were taken by surprise.

When the eruption stopped, Pompeii was buried under more than six meters of volcanic debris. The same ashes that destroyed the city also preserved evidence of daily life at that tragic moment. Pompeii was excavated at the end of the 18th century, and the city miraculously came to life again.

Pompeii's urban plan slightly differs from the rigid symmetry typical of other Roman towns. It looks more irregular at first glance, due both to the shape of the terrain and to the presence of pre-Roman elements. Archeologists divided the city into nine sections, delimited by the main streets (via di Nola, via dell'Abbondanza, via di Stabia), which correspond to what today would be called 'neighborhoods'. Each section is made up by insulae, or blocks, with numbered entrances.

The entrance to the city is through Porta Marina, one of six gates (Porta di Stabia, di Sarno, di Nola, Porta Vesuvio and Porta Ercolana) in the mighty walls encircling Pompeii.

The Central Forum.

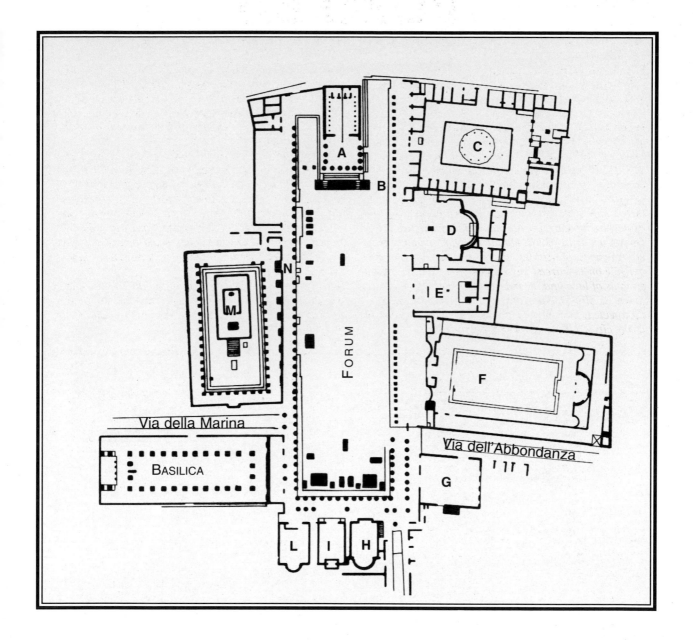

PLAN OF THE CENTRAL FORUM

A) Temple of Jupiter.
B) Arch of Tiberius.
C) Macellum.
D) Temple of the Lares.
E) Temple of Vespasian.
F) Building of Eumachia.

G) Comitium.
H) The Curia.
I)   Hall of the Duumviri.
L) Hall of the Aediles.
M) Temple of Apollo.
N) Mensa Ponderaria.

The Basilica.

THE PUBLIC BUILDINGS

To the right of the entrance of the *Porta Marina* is the **Antiquarium**, which preserves in chronological order works from the pre-Samnite period through the 1st century of the Roman Empire. The *Temple of Venus* follows, and further to the right, on Via Marina, is the **Basilica**, center of economic and judicial life, built in 120 AD. It is a rectangular building divided into three naves by robust columns in brick, while against the walls are half-columns surmounted by an entablature.

On the left are the remains of the **Temple of Apollo**, enclosed by 48 columns. The *cella* is set on a high podium surrounded by a Corinthian colonnade. Beneath the stairway is the *ara (altar)*, in travertine, whose inscription dates to the Republican era. The two bronze statues along the portico represent *Apollo Sagittarius and Diana*, copies of the masterpieces, which, like many others found during the excavations, are on display in the Museo Archeologico Nazionale in Naples.

The **Forum**, made up of a large rectangular piazza, was the center of the city's civic, religious and economic life. The north side is closed by the 2nd-century BC **Temple of Jupiter**, flanked by two honourary arches. The largest sacred building built in the city since the Samnite era, the

Temple of Apollo with the statue of Apollo Sagittarius.

Temple is a conspicuous example of Italic style, set on a podium with a double set of steps. It features a pronaos, encircled by Corinthian columns and a large cella with an internal colonnade (where the *Colossal Head of Jupiter*, now in the Museo Archeologico Nazionale in Naples, was found). The other three sides were encircled by a portico, built in the Samnite era, and partially restored in the Roman period. Several tracts of the portico were surmounted by a loggiato, with slender columns which ran above the entablature.

A series of bases on the south side marks the places of numerous honourary statues, while the largest pediment has been identified with the *suggestum*, the tribune of the orators. Beyond the portico on the east side of the piazza were: the *Macellum*, the covered market for food and staples (1st century AD); the *Temple of the Lares* (Lararium); the *Temple of Vespasian*, featuring the beautiful central altar with a relief representing a sacrificial scene; and the *Building of Eumachia*, built at the expense of the priestess Eumachia, as written in the inscription; large niches in the facade contained statues of the mythological and historical forefathers of the Julian family, which included Julius Caesar and Augustus. The large doorway features beautiful marble door jambs decorated with elegant reliefs. This building held the seat of the cloth dyers and washers guild. The Forum ended in the *Comitium*, the large room used for

The Temple of Jupiter.

electoral meetings which still contains the tribune upon which the magistrates watched over the electoral urn.

Nearby, the *Triangular Forum* contains the remains of the oldest cult area in Pompeii, the *Doric Temple* of the 6th century, dedicated to Hercules.

The **Large** or **Open theatre** (Teatro Grande) was built between 200 and 150 BC, and makes use of the natural cavity of the hill. In the Augustean era it held 50,000 spectators. The lower stands remain in a small portion of the middle part of the cavea (seating area), along with a part of the stage with niches and aediculae (shrines).

To the side rises the **Small theatre** or **Odeon**, built in the early Roman period (80-95 BC). It had a permanent roof, unlike the Teatro Grande, which was at times covered by a velarium (awning). The theatre, which was never renovated, presents a fine balance between structure and dec-oration, as easily seen in its well-preserved cavea.

On the far eastern side of the city is the **Amphitheater**, built against the city wall. Finished in about 80 BC, it is the oldest surviving example of its kind. At that time, the spectators came principally to see gladiator combat, and therefore the arena has no subterranean level, which became necessary in amphitheaters which hosted spectacles with wild beasts or sea battles, such as the Colosseum. The most important spectators sat in the first and second tiers, while a loggia which ran along the top of the cavea was reserved for women. A *velarium (awning)* protected the spectators and the arena from rain and excessive heat.

West of Piazza dell'Anfiteatro is a **palestra** (gymnasium) of enormous dimensions, encircled on three sides by a beautiful portico with Corinthian columns. In the center is a pool with a slanted bottom, once shaded by plane trees.

The Triangular Forum - Detail.

The Macellum.

The Large Theater.

The Amphitheater.

al *peristyles* (courtyards surrounded by columns).

The *Pompeian house in the Roman era* was generally a single family dwelling that was focused toward the interior. An entrance corridor *(vestibulum and fauces)* led to an atrium, half-covered by a roofed arcade which slanted toward the interior, with a rectangular basin at the center *(impluvium)* to collect rain water. At the end of the atrium was often a *tablinum*, which gave way to the *peristyle*, upon which various rooms opened. As the city grew, the Pompeian house in the Roman era tended to become smaller, but more decorated, with vividly coloured wall paintings. However, some prestigious houses belonging to the local aristocracy were quite vast (as large as 3000 square meters). Often decorated with mosaic or coloured marble floors, these noble houses, in many cases, had shops which opened onto the street, run by servants who sold the merchandise of their masters.

PRIVATE POMPEII

Pompeii's fame is above all connected with its private buildings. No other place in the world, with the exception of Herculaneum and Ostia Antica, presents such complete evidence about every aspect of private dwellings: from the structure, to the decoration, to the furnishings. The accurate restoration of the roofs gives a good idea of the original appearance of the Pompeian house.

Aside from the Roman-style house, there were also other types, like the *Italic house* from the Samnite era. It was completely set around an *atrium Tuscanicum*, at the end of which was the *tablinum*, the most sacred place of the house and meeting area for the family. A larger, more elegant type of house, clearly of Hellenistic influence, was set around sever-

The Gymnasium

The colonnade of the Forum.

Via dell'Abbondanza.

The Menanader.

VIA DELL'ABBONDANZA

Via dell'Abbondanza begins at the Forum and leads to Porta di Sarno. It takes its name from a fountain with a bas-relief of a lady with a cornucopia, symbol of abundance. Lively and prosperous, it was one of the most commercial streets in the city.

The **Villa of Julia Felix**, at the far end of the road, is so large that it occupies an entire insula (city block). It is divided in three parts: the dwelling of the proprietress, a public bathroom, and a section of rental apartments with separate entrances. The villa had, in addition, a beautiful porticoed garden, with a fishpond in the center, decorated by statues. The most important rooms of the house looked out onto the garden, among them the *triclinium (dining room)*, decorated by a still life, and a vast room with a fresco representing the *Nine Muses*. Both paintings were taken away during excavations in the 18th century; the first is on display at the Museo Archeologico Nazionale in Naples, while the second is in the Louvre in Paris.

The **House of Octavius Quartus** (or *House of Loreius Tiburtinus*) includes a *large triclinium*, decorated with scenes inspired by the Iliad and the story of Heraclides; and a vast room (probably dedicated to the cult of Isis), whose large scale decoration, made with impressive technical skill, represents one of the highest examples of Pompeiian painting of the *fourth style* (ornamentation based on illusion with architectonic prospective). Also interesting are the *long porticoed loggia* with an arbor, the little *temple* with four columns, and the long canal adorned with small marble sculptures.

The **House of the Lararium** takes its name from its most artistically important room, decorated in white stucco against a blue background, with extremely fine paintings of scenes from the Iliad.

The **House of Paquius Proculus** features a vestibule adorned with mosaics, one of which represents *a chained dog*. Beautiful *mosaics* in the Alexandrian style (with fine, tiny tesserae) also embellish the salon which faces onto the peristyle. Here were found the skeletons of seven children, killed in their attempt to find shelter in the course of the tragic eruption of Mt. Vesuvius.

On Vicolo Meridionale is the solemn entrance to the large **House of the Menander**, so-called because of the portrait of the Greek poet painted in one of the exedrae (recess) that opens onto the peristyle. The *atrium* is decorated with frescoes in the fourth Pompeian style. It leads to the *lararium*, in the shape small temple, and to an exedra, with precious paintings representing *three episodes of the fall of Troy*.

The peristyle is surrounded by richly coloured stuccoed columns, painted on the lower part in red and black, and delineated by a balustrade decorated with vegetable motifs and herons. The spaces inside the house are more luxurious: on the northern side, a room with elegant dec-

The House of the Lararium.

The House of Paquius Proculus.

The Central Baths.

The Stabian Baths. The apodyterium.

oration on a green background; the triclinium (dining room) on the east side; semi-circular and rectangular exedrae along the southern frescoed ambulatory; and the section of the bath on the western side, which preserves intact its fine mosaic, painting and stucco decoration.

The **House of the Cryptoporticus** features a covered portico (cryptoporticus), which the last owner was transforming into a wine cellar, as evidenced by the amphorae and partition walls. The inhabitants of the house sought refuge here, and their bodies, dramatically frozen at the moment of death, are on display in cases in a hall in the gallery.

VIA DI STABIA

This was another of Pompeii's commercial streets. In the first part, which comes from Via dell'Abbondanza, there were taverns, small hotels, shops, and bakeries (like *Modesto's bakery*). At the intersection are the **Stabian Baths**, the oldest and most complete in Pompeii. The entrance leads to a large *palestra* surrounded on three sides by a portico of Doric columns made of tufa dressed in stucco. On the eastern side of the *portico* were the **public baths**. The *men's section* presents a beautiful vestibule with barrel vaults, decorated with well-preserved, elegant stuccoes, and a dressing room, also covered with vaults and decorated in stucco. The vestibule leads to the *frigidarium*, on a round plan, with a domed vault and niches with marine paintings. The *tepidarium* and the *calidarium* follow. The latter was a large room with apses, decorated with extremely fine stucco friezes. The *women's section* presents an analogous subdivision and comparable level of decoration.

On the northern side of the portico were the **private baths**. The more modern section on the eastern side, reflects the later trend by which a bath was always accompanied by gymnastic exercises. A vast basin in the open air, surrounded by dressing rooms, here took the place of the small tub of the frigidarium.

The **Central Baths** were the most modern bath complex in Pompeii. Begun in 62 AD, they were still unfinished at the time of the eruption. These baths, too, were set around a central palaestra, with a swimming pool at the far end. On the southern side were the toilets and dressing areas; on the eastern side, the usual thermal rooms, larger and more airy than in the other baths, to which was added a new facility, the *laconicum*. This was a circular, domed room for sweating, in which the heat was drier and more intense than in the calidarium.

Nearby is the **Lupanare**, the best preserved brothel in the city. Built on two floors, it had five rooms on each floor. Each room on the first floor had beds upon which mattresses were placed.

The entrance wall of each room was frescoed, depicting the particular specialty of the prostitute.

The House of the Gilded Cupids.

BETWEEN THE VIA DI MERCURIO AND THE VIA DI STABIA

The **House of the Gilded Cupids** is a refined abode which belonged to the family of Poppea, wife of Nero. The small dimensions of the building and its irregular form emphasize the richness of the decorations and the abundance of the furnishings, which made this a quite opulent residence. The beautiful *peristyle* (with an elevated side) is at the center of the house, while the *garden* which extends toward the interior is filled with hermae (busts) and reliefs. On the north side is a *lararium* in the form of a small temple. The *triclinium* is finely decorated with paintings of mythological scenes in the third Pompeian style (also called the Egyptian or royal wall style). Also worthy of attention is the *cubiculum (bedroom)*, decorated with small glass discs with several *cupids* engraved in gold leaf.

The **House of the Vettii** is one of the best representations of the lavish taste of the Imperial era, in which Pompeii played an intense commercial role. The exterior of the building is in excellent condition. The *atrium* has a very intimate feeling, and is adorned by strong-boxes and a beautiful frieze of *Cupids and Psyches*. To the left of the atrium is a room with pictorial decorations: above, a *frieze with darting fish*; below, two small pictures which represent *Ariadne abandoned and Eros and Leander*. The next room is larger, and contains paintings, including *Cipressus*, shown at the moment of his metamorphosis into a cypress tree; and the *Battle between Pan and Eros*. Above, *inserted in a beautiful architectural decoration, is Jupiter Enthroned, Leda and Danae*.

Two wings depart from the atrium; the one on the left presents a scene from the *Battle of the Gauls*, the one on the right small *medallions with the heads of Medusa and Silenus*. The atrium leads directly to the peristyle, which along with the garden, is one of the highlights of this house. It was in fact possible to reconstruct the original designs of the *flower beds*, and the bronze and marble *statuettes* of the fountain were left in their original positions. The *triclinium* opens onto this lovely garden, which

The House of the Vettii.

allowed the inhabitants to eat while enjoying the fresh air. The room has red walls with black striping all around, originally framing a mythological scene, probably painted on canvas. The *frame* remains, with figures of *cupids* representing the arts and crafts, while on a wall are the recognizable figures of mythological subjects such as *Dionysius and Ariadne*, *Apollo and Daphne*, etc. Two splendidly decorated *oeci* (reception rooms) also open onto the peristyle.

The next arca was the most private of the house, probably the *gynaeceum or women's room*, made up of a tiny garden with a cubiculum (bedroom) and triclinium, decorated with paintings of *Ulysses recognizing Achilles in disguise and Hercules* and *Auge caught in the act of washing the peplum of Minerva*. Finally, passing to the *rustic quarter*,

we find a tiny *atrium* with a small impluvium and a *lararium* decorated in stucco; the *kitchen* looks onto a small courtyard.

The **House of Meleager** is an aristocratic dwelling that dates to the Samnite period, but with completely renovated pictorial decoration, which dates to the Roman era. In fact, it constitutes an interesting example of the Pompeian fourth style, above all in the decoration of a *vast triclinium* which faces the northwest corner of the peristyle. The latter features a beautiful Doric colonnade, at the center of which opens a large basin, which for its dimensions can be considered a true swimming pool. Three ample *reception rooms* open onto the eastern hall of the peristyle; the central room is rendered particularly solemn by a typically Hellenistic internal colonnade.

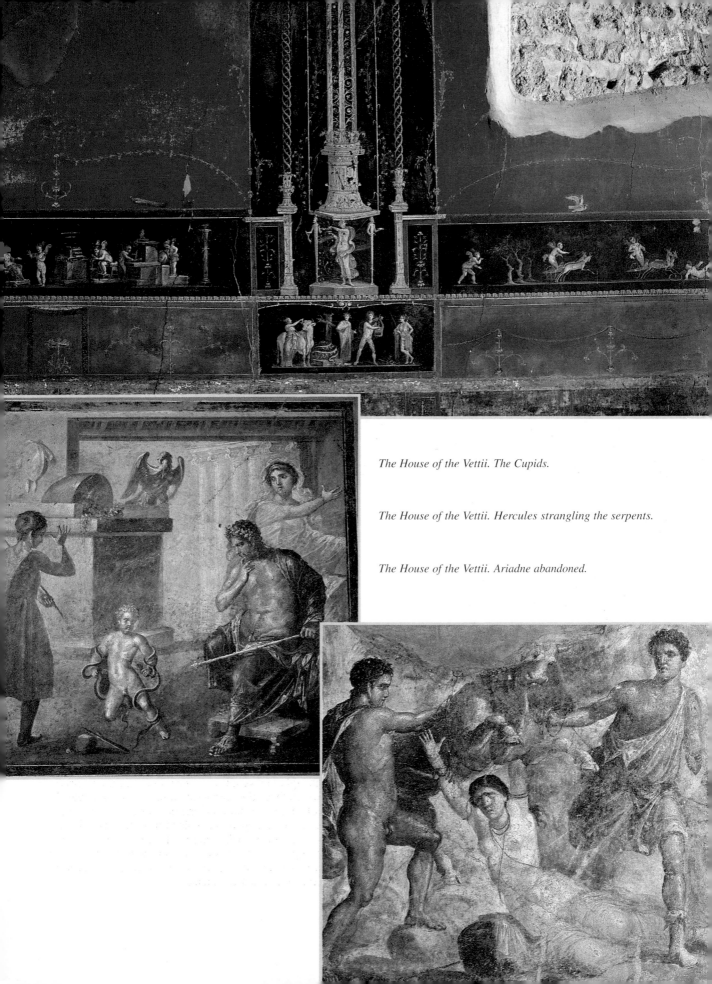

The House of the Vettii. The Cupids.

The House of the Vettii. Hercules strangling the serpents.

The House of the Vettii. Ariadne abandoned.

The **House of the Faun** is perhaps the most beautiful private dwelling that remains from the ancient world. The building dates to the Samnite era (2nd century BC) and appears typically Italic, although with some Hellenistic elements, especially the exceptional mosaic decoration (on display at the Museo Archeologico Nazionale in Naples).

The wall decorations of the vestibule feature two *lararii* in the form of a small temple, in extremely fine stucco; the floor is laid out in *opus sectile* with polychrome marble tiles. The *impluvium* leads to the two atriums at the center of the house. One is a typically Italic *atrium Tuscanicum*, while the other is an *atrium tetrastylum*, which is Hellenistic in form. The principle atrium is connected to the traditional tablinum, on the sides of which open two triclinii, used primarily in winter.

Next is the first peristyle, with twenty-eight Ionic style columns and a fountain at the center. In the background is an *exedra* with a floor that was originally made up of a splendid mosaic representing the *Battle between Alexander and Darius*, one of the most important of the Roman era, which gave the space a character of exceptional nobility and splendour.

The second and larger *peristyle* follows, with a Doric portico surmounted by a loggiato, at the end of which opens a back exit.

The Gardens and the House of the Faun.

The atrium of the House of the Faun, with the bronze statue of the Dancing Faun.

VIA DEI SEPOLCRI

The **Porta di Ercolano** (**Herculaneum Gate**), used by salt traders, was the most important in Pompeii. The gate features three arches; the central arch was reserved for carts, the side arches for pedestrians. From here begins the famous **Via dei Sepolcri** (**Street of the Tombs**), flanked by monumental tombs, prestigious villas, tabernae (wine shops and inns), all found in a perfect state of conservation.

The street leads to the **Villa of Diomede**s, an important house outside the city. Uncovered in excavations conducted between 1771 and 1774, it has a elaborate and complex plan, but is without decoration. Across the road is the **Villa of the Mysteries** particularly interesting not only from an architectural point of view, but also for its unique pictorial decoration. On a quadrilateral plan, it features a unusual structure: Today the entrance, on the opposite side as the original one, is through a large *exedra* at the center of a suspended terrace, with two symmetrical wings of a portico which face the countryside. The next room is the *tablinum*, which consists of a passageway with a beautiful miniature decoration with characters against a black background, to the right of which is a cubiculum with *figures of the Dionysian cult*. The adjacent large **Room of the Large Painting**, is connected to this same cult. The decoration is particularly striking, set against a vividly coloured background with large figures harmoniously grouped together, and completely different from other pictorial decorations in Pompeii. It represents, from left to right across three walls (beginning from the north wall), a complete cycle of ceremonial scenes.

Villa of the Mysteries. Veiled woman performing a sacrificial rite.

Villa of the Mysteries. Fresco cycle in the Sala del Grande Dipinto (of the large painting).

INDEX